Spark for Python Developers

A concise guide to implementing Spark big data analytics for Python developers and building a real-time and insightful trend tracker data-intensive app

FREDERICA,

MAY THE PYTHONIC
SPARK ENLIGHTEN
YOUR CODES

AMIT

Amit Nandi

[PACKT] open source *
PUBLISHING   community experience distilled

BIRMINGHAM - MUMBAI

Spark for Python Developers

First published: December 2015

Production reference: 1171215

Published by Packt Publishing Ltd.
Livery Place
35 Livery Street
Birmingham B3 2PB, UK.

ISBN 978-1-78439-969-6

www.packtpub.com

Credits

About the Author

Amit Nandi studied physics at the Free University of Brussels in Belgium, where he did his research on computer generated holograms. Computer generated holograms are the key components of an optical computer, which is powered by photons running at the speed of light. He then worked with the university Cray supercomputer, sending batch jobs of programs written in Fortran. This gave him a taste for computing, which kept growing. He has worked extensively on large business reengineering initiatives, using SAP as the main enabler. He focused for the last 15 years on start-ups in the data space, pioneering new areas of the information technology landscape. He is currently focusing on large-scale data-intensive applications as an enterprise architect, data engineer, and software developer. He understands and speaks seven human languages. Although Python is his computer language of choice, he aims to be able to write fluently in seven computer languages too.

Acknowledgment

I want to express my profound gratitude to my parents for their unconditional love and strong support in all my endeavors.

This book arose from an initial discussion with Richard Gall, an acquisition editor at Packt Publishing. Without this initial discussion, this book would never have happened. So, I am grateful to him. The follow ups on discussions and the contractual terms were agreed with Rebecca Youe. I would like to thank her for her support. I would also like to thank Merint Mathew, a content editor who helped me bring this book to the finish line. I am thankful to Merint for his subtle persistence and tactful support during the write ups and revisions of this book.

We are standing on the shoulders of giants. I want to acknowledge some of the giants who helped me shape my thinking. I want to recognize the beauty, elegance, and power of Python as envisioned by Guido van Rossum. My respectful gratitude goes to Matei Zaharia and the team at Berkeley AMP Lab and Databricks for developing a new approach to computing with Spark and Mesos. Travis Oliphant, Peter Wang, and the team at Continuum.io are doing a tremendous job of keeping Python relevant in a fast-changing computing landscape. Thank you to you all.

About the Reviewers

Manuel Ignacio Franco Galeano is a software developer from Colombia. He holds a computer science degree from the University of Quindío. At the moment of publication of this book, he was studying to get his MSc in computer science from University College Dublin, Ireland. He has a wide range of interests that include distributed systems, machine learning, micro services, and so on. He is looking for a way to apply machine learning techniques to audio data in order to help people learn more about music.

Rahul Kavale works as a software developer at TinyOwl Ltd. He is interested in multiple technologies ranging from building web applications to solving big data problems. He has worked in multiple languages, including Scala, Ruby, and Java, and has worked on Apache Spark, Apache Storm, Apache Kafka, Hadoop, and Hive. He enjoys writing Scala. Functional programming and distributed computing are his areas of interest. He has been using Spark since its early stage for varying use cases. He has also helped with the review for the *Pragmatic Scala* book.

Daniel Lemire has a BSc and MSc in mathematics from the University of Toronto and a PhD in engineering mathematics from the Ecole Polytechnique and the Université de Montréal. He is a professor of computer science at the Université du Québec. He has also been a research officer at the National Research Council of Canada and an entrepreneur. He has written over 45 peer-reviewed publications, including more than 25 journal articles. He has held competitive research grants for the last 15 years. He has been an expert on several committees with funding agencies (NSERC and FQRNT). He has served as a program committee member on leading computer science conferences (for example, ACM CIKM, ACM WSDM, ACM SIGIR, and ACM RecSys). His open source software has been used by major corporations such as Google and Facebook. His research interests include databases, information retrieval and high-performance programming. He blogs regularly on computer science at `http://lemire.me/blog/`.

Chet Mancini is a data engineer at Intent Media, Inc in New York, where he works with the data science team to store and process terabytes of web travel data to build predictive models of shopper behavior. He enjoys functional programming, immutable data structures, and machine learning. He writes and speaks on topics surrounding data engineering and information architecture.

He is a contributor to Apache Spark and other libraries in the Spark ecosystem. Chet has a master's degree in computer science from Cornell University.

www.PacktPub.com

Support files, eBooks, discount offers, and more

For support files and downloads related to your book, please visit www.PacktPub.com.

Did you know that Packt offers eBook versions of every book published, with PDF and ePub files available? You can upgrade to the eBook version at www.PacktPub.com and as a print book customer, you are entitled to a discount on the eBook copy. Get in touch with us at service@packtpub.com for more details.

At www.PacktPub.com, you can also read a collection of free technical articles, sign up for a range of free newsletters and receive exclusive discounts and offers on Packt books and eBooks.

https://www2.packtpub.com/books/subscription/packtlib

Do you need instant solutions to your IT questions? PacktLib is Packt's online digital book library. Here, you can search, access, and read Packt's entire library of books.

Why subscribe?

- Fully searchable across every book published by Packt
- Copy and paste, print, and bookmark content
- On demand and accessible via a web browser

Free access for Packt account holders

If you have an account with Packt at www.PacktPub.com, you can use this to access PacktLib today and view 9 entirely free books. Simply use your login credentials for immediate access.

Table of Contents

Preface

Spark for Python Developers aims to combine the elegance and flexibility of Python with the power and versatility of Apache Spark. Spark is written in Scala and runs on the Java virtual machine. It is nevertheless polyglot and offers bindings and APIs for Java, Scala, Python, and R. Python is a well-designed language with an extensive set of specialized libraries. This book looks at PySpark within the PyData ecosystem. Some of the prominent PyData libraries include Pandas, Blaze, Scikit-Learn, Matplotlib, Seaborn, and Bokeh. These libraries are open source. They are developed, used, and maintained by the data scientist and Python developers community. PySpark integrates well with the PyData ecosystem, as endorsed by the Anaconda Python distribution. The book puts forward a journey to build data-intensive apps along with an architectural blueprint that covers the following steps: first, set up the base infrastructure with Spark. Second, acquire, collect, process, and store the data. Third, gain insights from the collected data. Fourth, stream live data and process it in real time. Finally, visualize the information.

The objective of the book is to learn about PySpark and PyData libraries by building apps that analyze the Spark community's interactions on social networks. The focus is on Twitter data.

What this book covers

Chapter 1, Setting Up a Spark Virtual Environment, covers how to create a segregated virtual machine as our sandbox or development environment to experiment with Spark and PyData libraries. It covers how to install Spark and the Python Anaconda distribution, which includes PyData libraries. Along the way, we explain the key Spark concepts, the Python Anaconda ecosystem, and build a Spark word count app.

Chapter 2, *Building Batch and Streaming Apps with Spark*, lays the foundation of the *Data Intensive Apps Architecture*. It describes the five layers of the apps architecture blueprint: infrastructure, persistence, integration, analytics, and engagement. We establish API connections with three social networks: Twitter, GitHub, and Meetup. This chapter provides the tools to connect to these three nontrivial APIs so that you can create your own data mashups at a later stage.

Chapter 3, *Juggling Data with Spark*, covers how to harvest data from Twitter and process it using Pandas, Blaze, and SparkSQL with their respective implementations of the dataframe data structure. We proceed with further investigations and techniques using Spark SQL, leveraging on the Spark dataframe data structure.

Chapter 4, *Learning from Data Using Spark*, gives an overview of the ever expanding library of algorithms of Spark MLlib. It covers supervised and unsupervised learning, recommender systems, optimization, and feature extraction algorithms. We put the Twitter harvested dataset through a Python Scikit-Learn and Spark MLlib K-means clustering in order to segregate the *Apache Spark* relevant tweets.

Chapter 5, *Streaming Live Data with Spark*, lays down the foundation of streaming architecture apps and describes their challenges, constraints, and benefits. We illustrate the streaming concepts with TCP sockets, followed by live tweet ingestion and processing directly from the Twitter firehose. We also describe Flume, a reliable, flexible, and scalable data ingestion and transport pipeline system. The combination of Flume, Kafka, and Spark delivers unparalleled robustness, speed, and agility in an ever-changing landscape. We end the chapter with some remarks and observations on two streaming architectural paradigms, the Lambda and Kappa architectures.

Chapter 6, *Visualizing Insights and Trends*, focuses on a few key visualization techniques. It covers how to build word clouds and expose their intuitive power to reveal a lot of the key words, moods, and memes carried through thousands of tweets. We then focus on interactive mapping visualizations using Bokeh. We build a world map from the ground up and create a scatter plot of critical tweets. Our final visualization is to overlay an actual Google map of London, highlighting upcoming meetups and their respective topics.

What you need for this book

You need inquisitiveness, perseverance, and passion for data, software engineering, application architecture and scalability, and beautiful succinct visualizations. The scope is broad and wide.

You need a good understanding of Python or a similar language with object-oriented and functional programming capabilities. Preliminary experience of data wrangling with Python, R, or any similar tool is helpful.

You need to appreciate how to conceive, build, and scale data applications.

Who this book is for

The target audience includes the following:

- Data scientists are the primary interested parties. This book will help you unleash the power of Spark and leverage your Python, R, and machine learning background.

- Software developers with a focus on Python will readily expand their skills to create data-intensive apps using Spark as a processing engine and Python visualization libraries and web frameworks.

- Data architects who can create rapid data pipelines and build the famous Lambda architecture that encompasses batch and streaming processing to render insights on data in real time, using the Spark and Python rich ecosystem, will also benefit from this book.

Conventions

In this book, you will find a number of styles of text that distinguish between different kinds of information. Here are some examples of these styles, and an explanation of their meaning.

Code words in text, database table names, folder names, filenames, file extensions, pathnames, dummy URLs, user input, and Twitter handles are shown as follows "Launch PySpark with IPYNB in directory examples/AN_Spark where the Jupyter or IPython Notebooks are stored".

A block of code is set as follows:

```
# Word count on 1st Chapter of the Book using PySpark

# import regex module
import re
# import add from operator module
from operator import add


# read input file
file_in = sc.textFile('/home/an/Documents/A00_Documents/Spark4Py
20150315')
```

Any command-line input or output is written as follows:

```
# install anaconda 2.x.x
bash Anaconda-2.x.x-Linux-x86[_64].sh
```

New terms and **important words** are shown in bold. Words that you see on the screen, in menus or dialog boxes for example, appear in the text like this: "After installing VirtualBox, let's open the Oracle VM VirtualBox Manager and click the **New** button."

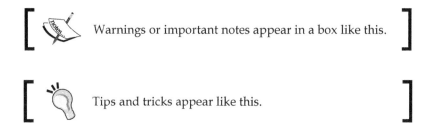

Warnings or important notes appear in a box like this.

Tips and tricks appear like this.

Reader feedback

Feedback from our readers is always welcome. Let us know what you think about this book—what you liked or may have disliked. Reader feedback is important for us to develop titles that you really get the most out of.

To send us general feedback, simply send an e-mail to feedback@packtpub.com, and mention the book title via the subject of your message.

If there is a topic that you have expertise in and you are interested in either writing or contributing to a book, see our author guide on www.packtpub.com/authors.

Customer support

Now that you are the proud owner of a Packt book, we have a number of things to help you to get the most from your purchase.

Downloading the example code

You can download the example code files for all Packt books you have purchased from your account at http://www.packtpub.com. If you purchased this book elsewhere, you can visit http://www.packtpub.com/support and register to have the files e-mailed directly to you.

Errata

Although we have taken every care to ensure the accuracy of our content, mistakes do happen. If you find a mistake in one of our books—maybe a mistake in the text or the code—we would be grateful if you would report this to us. By doing so, you can save other readers from frustration and help us improve subsequent versions of this book. If you find any errata, please report them by visiting http://www.packtpub.com/submit-errata, selecting your book, clicking on the **errata submission form** link, and entering the details of your errata. Once your errata are verified, your submission will be accepted and the errata will be uploaded on our website, or added to any list of existing errata, under the Errata section of that title. Any existing errata can be viewed by selecting your title from http://www.packtpub.com/support.

Piracy

Piracy of copyright material on the Internet is an ongoing problem across all media. At Packt, we take the protection of our copyright and licenses very seriously. If you come across any illegal copies of our works, in any form, on the Internet, please provide us with the location address or website name immediately so that we can pursue a remedy.

Please contact us at copyright@packtpub.com with a link to the suspected pirated material.

We appreciate your help in protecting our authors, and our ability to bring you valuable content.

Questions

You can contact us at questions@packtpub.com if you are having a problem with any aspect of the book, and we will do our best to address it.

1
Setting Up a Spark Virtual Environment

In this chapter, we will build an isolated virtual environment for development purposes. The environment will be powered by Spark and the PyData libraries provided by the Python Anaconda distribution. These libraries include Pandas, Scikit-Learn, Blaze, Matplotlib, Seaborn, and Bokeh. We will perform the following activities:

- Setting up the development environment using the Anaconda Python distribution. This will include enabling the IPython Notebook environment powered by PySpark for our data exploration tasks.

- Installing and enabling Spark, and the PyData libraries such as Pandas, Scikit- Learn, Blaze, Matplotlib, and Bokeh.

- Building a `word count` example app to ensure that everything is working fine.

The last decade has seen the rise and dominance of data-driven behemoths such as Amazon, Google, Twitter, LinkedIn, and Facebook. These corporations, by seeding, sharing, or disclosing their infrastructure concepts, software practices, and data processing frameworks, have fostered a vibrant open source software community. This has transformed the enterprise technology, systems, and software architecture.

This includes new infrastructure and DevOps (short for development and operations), concepts leveraging virtualization, cloud technology, and software-defined networks.

To process petabytes of data, Hadoop was developed and open sourced, taking its inspiration from the **Google File System (GFS)** and the adjoining distributed computing framework, MapReduce. Overcoming the complexities of scaling while keeping costs under control has also led to a proliferation of new data stores. Examples of recent database technology include Cassandra, a columnar database; MongoDB, a document database; and Neo4J, a graph database.

Hadoop, thanks to its ability to process huge datasets, has fostered a vast ecosystem to query data more iteratively and interactively with Pig, Hive, Impala, and Tez. Hadoop is cumbersome as it operates only in batch mode using MapReduce. Spark is creating a revolution in the analytics and data processing realm by targeting the shortcomings of disk input-output and bandwidth-intensive MapReduce jobs.

Spark is written in Scala, and therefore integrates natively with the **Java Virtual Machine (JVM)** powered ecosystem. Spark had early on provided Python API and bindings by enabling PySpark. The Spark architecture and ecosystem is inherently polyglot, with an obvious strong presence of Java-led systems.

This book will focus on PySpark and the PyData ecosystem. Python is one of the preferred languages in the academic and scientific community for data-intensive processing. Python has developed a rich ecosystem of libraries and tools in data manipulation with Pandas and Blaze, in Machine Learning with Scikit-Learn, and in data visualization with Matplotlib, Seaborn, and Bokeh. Hence, the aim of this book is to build an end-to-end architecture for data-intensive applications powered by Spark and Python. In order to put these concepts in to practice, we will analyze social networks such as Twitter, GitHub, and Meetup. We will focus on the activities and social interactions of Spark and the Open Source Software community by tapping into GitHub, Twitter, and Meetup.

Building data-intensive applications requires highly scalable infrastructure, polyglot storage, seamless data integration, multiparadigm analytics processing, and efficient visualization. The following paragraph describes the data-intensive app architecture blueprint that we will adopt throughout the book. It is the backbone of the book. We will discover Spark in the context of the broader PyData ecosystem.

Downloading the example code

You can download the example code files for all Packt books you have purchased from your account at http://www.packtpub.com. If you purchased this book elsewhere, you can visit http://www.packtpub.com/support and register to have the files e-mailed directly to you.

Understanding the architecture of data-intensive applications

In order to understand the architecture of data-intensive applications, the following conceptual framework is used. The is architecture is designed on the following five layers:

- Infrastructure layer
- Persistence layer
- Integration layer
- Analytics layer
- Engagement layer

The following screenshot depicts the five layers of the **Data Intensive App Framework**:

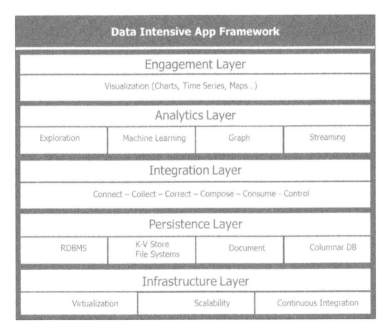

From the bottom up, let's go through the layers and their main purpose.

Infrastructure layer

The infrastructure layer is primarily concerned with virtualization, scalability, and continuous integration. In practical terms, and in terms of virtualization, we will go through building our own development environment in a VirtualBox and virtual machine powered by Spark and the Anaconda distribution of Python. If we wish to scale from there, we can create a similar environment in the cloud. The practice of creating a segregated development environment and moving into test and production deployment can be automated and can be part of a continuous integration cycle powered by DevOps tools such as **Vagrant**, **Chef**, **Puppet**, and **Docker**. Docker is a very popular open source project that eases the installation and deployment of new environments. The book will be limited to building the virtual machine using VirtualBox. From a data-intensive app architecture point of view, we are describing the essential steps of the infrastructure layer by mentioning scalability and continuous integration beyond just virtualization.

Persistence layer

The persistence layer manages the various repositories in accordance with data needs and shapes. It ensures the set up and management of the polyglot data stores. It includes relational database management systems such as **MySQL** and **PostgreSQL**; key-value data stores such as **Hadoop**, **Riak**, and **Redis**; columnar databases such as **HBase** and **Cassandra**; document databases such as **MongoDB** and **Couchbase**; and graph databases such as **Neo4j**. The persistence layer manages various filesystems such as Hadoop's HDFS. It interacts with various storage systems from native hard drives to Amazon S3. It manages various file storage formats such as `csv`, `json`, and `parquet`, which is a column-oriented format.

Integration layer

The integration layer focuses on data acquisition, transformation, quality, persistence, consumption, and governance. It is essentially driven by the following five Cs: *connect*, *collect*, *correct*, *compose*, and *consume*.

The five steps describe the lifecycle of data. They are focused on how to acquire the dataset of interest, explore it, iteratively refine and enrich the collected information, and get it ready for consumption. So, the steps perform the following operations:

- **Connect**: Targets the best way to acquire data from the various data sources, APIs offered by these sources, the input format, input schemas if they exist, the rate of data collection, and limitations from providers

- **Correct**: Focuses on transforming data for further processing and also ensures that the quality and consistency of the data received are maintained

- **Collect**: Looks at which data to store where and in what format, to ease data composition and consumption at later stages

- **Compose**: Concentrates its attention on how to mash up the various data sets collected, and enrich the information in order to build a compelling data-driven product

- **Consume**: Takes care of data provisioning and rendering and how the right data reaches the right individual at the right time

- **Control**: This sixth *additional* step will sooner or later be required as the data, the organization, and the participants grow and it is about ensuring data governance

The following diagram depicts the iterative process of data acquisition and refinement for consumption:

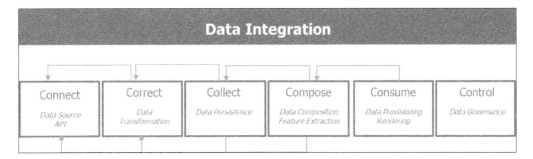

Analytics layer

The analytics layer is where Spark processes data with the various models, algorithms, and machine learning pipelines in order to derive insights. For our purpose, in this book, the analytics layer is powered by Spark. We will delve deeper in subsequent chapters into the merits of Spark. In a nutshell, what makes it so powerful is that it allows multiple paradigms of analytics processing in a single unified platform. It allows batch, streaming, and interactive analytics. Batch processing on large datasets with longer latency periods allows us to extract patterns and insights that can feed into real-time events in streaming mode. Interactive and iterative analytics are more suited for data exploration. Spark offers bindings and APIs in Python and R. With its **SparkSQL** module and the Spark Dataframe, it offers a very familiar analytics interface.

Engagement layer

The engagement layer interacts with the end user and provides dashboards, interactive visualizations, and alerts. We will focus here on the tools provided by the PyData ecosystem such as Matplotlib, Seaborn, and Bokeh.

Understanding Spark

Hadoop scales horizontally as the data grows. Hadoop runs on commodity hardware, so it is cost-effective. Intensive data applications are enabled by scalable, distributed processing frameworks that allow organizations to analyze petabytes of data on large commodity clusters. Hadoop is the first open source implementation of map-reduce. Hadoop relies on a distributed framework for storage called **HDFS (Hadoop Distributed File System)**. Hadoop runs map-reduce tasks in batch jobs. Hadoop requires persisting the data to disk at each map, shuffle, and reduce process step. The overhead and the latency of such batch jobs adversely impact the performance.

Spark is a fast, distributed general analytics computing engine for large-scale data processing. The major breakthrough from Hadoop is that Spark allows data sharing between processing steps through in-memory processing of data pipelines.

Spark is unique in that it allows four different styles of data analysis and processing. Spark can be used in:

- **Batch**: This mode is used for manipulating large datasets, typically performing large map-reduce jobs

- **Streaming**: This mode is used to process incoming information in near real time

- **Iterative**: This mode is for machine learning algorithms such as a gradient descent where the data is accessed repetitively in order to reach convergence

- **Interactive**: This mode is used for data exploration as large chunks of data are in memory and due to the very quick response time of Spark

The following figure highlights the preceding four processing styles:

Spark Processing Styles			
Batch	Iterative	Interactive	Streaming
High Throughput	*Convex Optimization*	*Low Latency*	*Continuous Processing*
Spark			

Spark operates in three modes: one single mode, standalone on a single machine and two distributed modes on a cluster of machines—on Yarn, the Hadoop distributed resource manager, or on Mesos, the open source cluster manager developed at Berkeley concurrently with Spark:

Spark Components			
Spark SQL	Spark MLLIB	Spark Streaming	Spark GraphX
Spark Core			
Standalone	Yarn		Mesos

Spark offers a polyglot interface in Scala, Java, Python, and R.

Spark libraries

Spark comes with batteries included, with some powerful libraries:

- **SparkSQL**: This provides the SQL-like ability to interrogate structured data and interactively explore large datasets
- **SparkMLLIB**: This provides major algorithms and a pipeline framework for machine learning
- **Spark Streaming**: This is for near real-time analysis of data using micro batches and sliding widows on incoming streams of data
- **Spark GraphX**: This is for graph processing and computation on complex connected entities and relationships

PySpark in action

Spark is written in Scala. The whole Spark ecosystem naturally leverages the JVM environment and capitalizes on HDFS natively. Hadoop HDFS is one of the many data stores supported by Spark. Spark is agnostic and from the beginning interacted with multiple data sources, types, and formats.

PySpark is not a transcribed version of Spark on a Java-enabled dialect of Python such as Jython. PySpark provides integrated API bindings around Spark and enables full usage of the Python ecosystem within all the nodes of the cluster with the pickle Python serialization and, more importantly, supplies access to the rich ecosystem of Python's machine learning libraries such as Scikit-Learn or data processing such as Pandas.

When we initialize a Spark program, the first thing a Spark program must do is to create a SparkContext object. It tells Spark how to access the cluster. The Python program creates a PySparkContext. Py4J is the gateway that binds the Python program to the Spark JVM SparkContext. The JVM SparkContextserializes the application codes and the closures and sends them to the cluster for execution. The cluster manager allocates resources and schedules, and ships the closures to the Spark workers in the cluster who activate Python virtual machines as required. In each machine, the Spark Worker is managed by an executor that controls computation, storage, and cache.

Here's an example of how the Spark driver manages both the PySpark context and the Spark context with its local filesystems and its interactions with the Spark worker through the cluster manager:

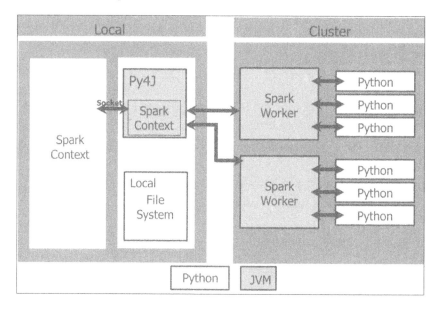

The Resilient Distributed Dataset

Spark applications consist of a driver program that runs the user's main function, creates distributed datasets on the cluster, and executes various parallel operations (transformations and actions) on those datasets.

Spark applications are run as an independent set of processes, coordinated by a SparkContext in a driver program.

The SparkContext will be allocated system resources (machines, memory, CPU) from the **Cluster manager**.

The `SparkContext` manages executors who manage workers in the cluster. The driver program has Spark jobs that need to run. The jobs are split into tasks submitted to the executor for completion. The executor takes care of computation, storage, and caching in each machine.

The key building block in Spark is the **RDD (Resilient Distributed Dataset)**. A dataset is a collection of elements. Distributed means the dataset can be on any node in the cluster. Resilient means that the dataset could get lost or partially lost without major harm to the computation in progress as Spark will re-compute from the data lineage in memory, also known as the **DAG** (short for **Directed Acyclic Graph**) of operations. Basically, Spark will snapshot in memory a state of the RDD in the cache. If one of the computing machines crashes during operation, Spark rebuilds the RDDs from the cached RDD and the DAG of operations. RDDs recover from node failure.

There are two types of operation on RDDs:

- **Transformations**: A transformation takes an existing RDD and leads to a pointer of a new transformed RDD. An RDD is immutable. Once created, it cannot be changed. Each transformation creates a new RDD. Transformations are lazily evaluated. Transformations are executed only when an action occurs. In the case of failure, the data lineage of transformations rebuilds the RDD.

- **Actions**: An action on an RDD triggers a Spark job and yields a value. An action operation causes Spark to execute the (lazy) transformation operations that are required to compute the RDD returned by the action. The action results in a DAG of operations. The DAG is compiled into stages where each stage is executed as a series of tasks. A task is a fundamental unit of work.

Here's some useful information on RDDs:

- RDDs are created from a data source such as an HDFS file or a DB query. There are three ways to create an RDD:
    - Reading from a datastore
    - Transforming an existing RDD
    - Using an in-memory collection

- RDDs are transformed with functions such as `map` or `filter`, which yield new RDDs.

- An action such as first, take, collect, or count on an RDD will deliver the results into the Spark driver. The Spark driver is the client through which the user interacts with the Spark cluster.

The following diagram illustrates the RDD transformation and action:

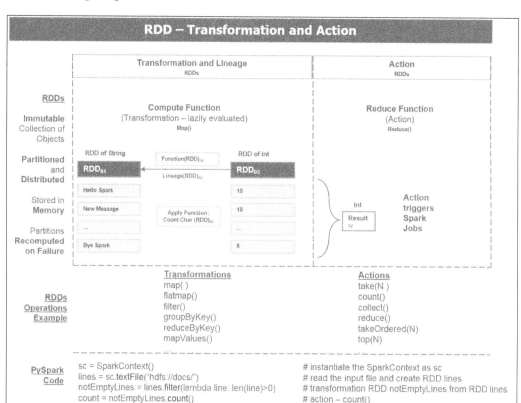

Understanding Anaconda

Anaconda is a widely used free Python distribution maintained by **Continuum** (`https://www.continuum.io/`). We will use the prevailing software stack provided by Anaconda to generate our apps. In this book, we will use PySpark and the PyData ecosystem. The PyData ecosystem is promoted, supported, and maintained by **Continuum** and powered by the **Anaconda** Python distribution. The Anaconda Python distribution essentially saves time and aggravation in the installation of the Python environment; we will use it in conjunction with Spark. Anaconda has its own package management that supplements the traditional `pip install` and `easy-install`. Anaconda comes with batteries included, namely some of the most important packages such as Pandas, Scikit-Learn, Blaze, Matplotlib, and Bokeh. An upgrade to any of the installed library is a simple command at the console:

```
$ conda update
```

A list of installed libraries in our environment can be obtained with command:

```
$ conda list
```

The key components of the stack are as follows:

- **Anaconda**: This is a free Python distribution with almost 200 Python packages for science, math, engineering, and data analysis.
- **Conda**: This is a package manager that takes care of all the dependencies of installing a complex software stack. This is not restricted to Python and manages the install process for R and other languages.
- **Numba**: This provides the power to speed up code in Python with high-performance functions and just-in-time compilation.
- **Blaze**: This enables large scale data analytics by offering a uniform and adaptable interface to access a variety of data providers, which include streaming Python, Pandas, SQLAlchemy, and Spark.
- **Bokeh**: This provides interactive data visualizations for large and streaming datasets.
- **Wakari**: This allows us to share and deploy IPython Notebooks and other apps on a hosted environment.

The following figure shows the components of the Anaconda stack:

Setting up the Spark powered environment

In this section, we will learn to set up Spark:

- Create a segregated development environment in a virtual machine running on Ubuntu 14.04, so it does not interfere with any existing system.
- Install Spark 1.3.0 with its dependencies, namely.
- Install the Anaconda Python 2.7 environment with all the required libraries such as Pandas, Scikit-Learn, Blaze, and Bokeh, and enable PySpark, so it can be accessed through IPython Notebooks.
- Set up the backend or data stores of our environment. We will use MySQL as the relational database, MongoDB as the document store, and Cassandra as the columnar database.

Each storage backend serves a specific purpose depending on the nature of the data to be handled. The MySQL RDBMs is used for standard tabular processed information that can be easily queried using SQL. As we will be processing a lot of JSON-type data from various APIs, the easiest way to store them is in a document. For real-time and time-series-related information, Cassandra is best suited as a columnar database.

The following diagram gives a view of the environment we will build and use throughout the book:

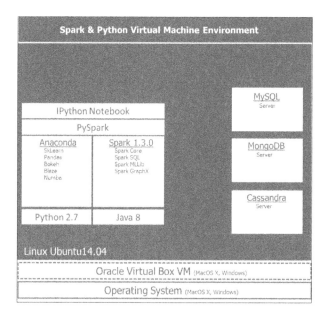

Setting up an Oracle VirtualBox with Ubuntu

Setting up a clean new VirtualBox environment on Ubuntu 14.04 is the safest way to create a development environment that does not conflict with existing libraries and can be later replicated in the cloud using a similar list of commands.

In order to set up an environment with Anaconda and Spark, we will create a VirtualBox virtual machine running Ubuntu 14.04.

Let's go through the steps of using VirtualBox with Ubuntu:

1. Oracle VirtualBox VM is free and can be downloaded from
   `https://www.virtualbox.org/wiki/Downloads`. The installation
   is pretty straightforward.

2. After installing VirtualBox, let's open the Oracle VM VirtualBox Manager
   and click the **New** button.

3. We'll give the new VM a name, and select Type **Linux** and Version **Ubuntu
   (64 bit)**.

4. You need to download the ISO from the Ubuntu website and allocate
   sufficient RAM (4 GB recommended) and disk space (20 GB recommended).
   We will use the Ubuntu 14.04.1 LTS release, which is found here: `http://
   www.ubuntu.com/download/desktop`.

5. Once the installation completed, it is advisable to install the VirtualBox
   Guest Additions by going to (from the VirtualBox menu, with the new VM
   running) **Devices | Insert Guest Additions CD image**. Failing to provide the
   guest additions in a Windows host gives a very limited user interface with
   reduced window sizes.

6. Once the additional installation completes, reboot the VM, and it will be
   ready to use. It is helpful to enable the shared clipboard by selecting the VM
   and clicking **Settings**, then go to **General | Advanced | Shared Clipboard**
   and click on **Bidirectional**.

Installing Anaconda with Python 2.7

PySpark currently runs only on Python 2.7. (There are requests from the community to upgrade to Python 3.3.) To install Anaconda, follow these steps:

1. Download the Anaconda Installer for Linux 64-bit Python 2.7 from
   `http://continuum.io/downloads#all`.

2. After downloading the Anaconda installer, open a terminal and navigate to the directory or folder where the installer has been saved. From here, run the following command, replacing the `2.x.x` in the command with the version number of the downloaded installer file:

```
# install anaconda 2.x.x
bash Anaconda-2.x.x-Linux-x86[_64].sh
```

3. After accepting the license terms, you will be asked to specify the install location (which `defaults to ~/anaconda`).

4. After the self-extraction is finished, you should add the anaconda binary directory to your PATH environment variable:

```
# add anaconda to PATH
bash Anaconda-2.x.x-Linux-x86[_64].sh
```

Installing Java 8

Spark runs on the JVM and requires the Java **SDK** (short for **Software Development Kit**) and not the **JRE** (short for **Java Runtime Environment**), as we will build apps with Spark. The recommended version is Java Version 7 or higher. Java 8 is the most suitable, as it includes many of the functional programming techniques available with Scala and Python.

To install Java 8, follow these steps:

1. Install Oracle Java 8 using the following commands:

```
# install oracle java 8
$ sudo apt-get install software-properties-common
$ sudo add-apt-repository ppa:webupd8team/java
$ sudo apt-get update
$ sudo apt-get install oracle-java8-installer
```

2. Set the `JAVA_HOME` environment variable and ensure that the Java program is on your PATH.

3. Check that `JAVA_HOME` is properly installed:

```
#
$ echo JAVA_HOME
```

Installing Spark

Head over to the Spark download page at `http://spark.apache.org/downloads.html`.

The Spark download page offers the possibility to download earlier versions of Spark and different package and download types. We will select the latest release, pre-built for Hadoop 2.6 and later. The easiest way to install Spark is to use a Spark package prebuilt for Hadoop 2.6 and later, rather than build it from source. Move the file to the directory `~/spark` under the root directory.

Download the latest release of Spark — Spark 1.5.2, released on November 9, 2015:

1. Select Spark release **1.5.2 (Nov 09 2015),**
2. Chose the package type **Prebuilt for Hadoop 2.6 and later,**
3. Chose the download type **Direct Download,**
4. Download Spark: **spark-1.5.2-bin-hadoop2.6.tgz,**
5. Verify this release using the 1.3.0 signatures and checksums,

This can also be accomplished by running:

```
# download spark
$ wget http://d3kbcqa49mib13.cloudfront.net/spark-1.5.2-bin-hadoop2.6.tgz
```

Next, we'll extract the files and clean up:

```
# extract, clean up, move the unzipped files under the spark directory
$ tar -xf spark-1.5.2-bin-hadoop2.6.tgz
$ rm spark-1.5.2-bin-hadoop2.6.tgz
$ sudo mv spark-* spark
```

Now, we can run the Spark Python interpreter with:

```
# run spark
$ cd ~/spark
./bin/pyspark
```

You should see something like this:

```
Welcome to

      ____              __
     / __/__  ___ _____/ /__
    _\ \/ _ \/ _ `/ __/  '_/
   /__ / .__/\_,_/_/ /_/\_\   version 1.5.2
      /_/

Using Python version 2.7.6 (default, Mar 22 2014 22:59:56)
SparkContext available as sc.
>>>
```

The interpreter will have already provided us with a Spark context object, sc, which we can see by running:

```
>>> print(sc)
<pyspark.context.SparkContext object at 0x7f34b61c4e50>
```

Enabling IPython Notebook

We will work with IPython Notebook for a friendlier user experience than the console.

You can launch IPython Notebook by using the following command:

```
$ IPYTHON_OPTS="notebook --pylab inline"  ./bin/pyspark
```

Launch PySpark with IPYNB in the directory examples/AN_Spark where Jupyter or IPython Notebooks are stored:

```
# cd to   /home/an/spark/spark-1.5.0-bin-hadoop2.6/examples/AN_Spark

# launch command using python 2.7 and the spark-csv package:
$ IPYTHON_OPTS='notebook' /home/an/spark/spark-1.5.0-bin-hadoop2.6/bin/
pyspark --packages com.databricks:spark-csv_2.11:1.2.0


# launch command using python 3.4 and the spark-csv package:
$ IPYTHON_OPTS='notebook' PYSPARK_PYTHON=python3

 /home/an/spark/spark-1.5.0-bin-hadoop2.6/bin/pyspark --packages com.
databricks:spark-csv_2.11:1.2.0
```

Building our first app with PySpark

We are ready to check now that everything is working fine. The obligatory word count will be put to the test in processing a word count on the first chapter of this book.

The code we will be running is listed here:

```python
# Word count on 1st Chapter of the Book using PySpark

# import regex module
import re
# import add from operator module
from operator import add


# read input file
file_in = sc.textFile('/home/an/Documents/A00_Documents/Spark4Py
20150315')

# count lines
print('number of lines in file: %s' % file_in.count())

# add up lengths of each line
chars = file_in.map(lambda s: len(s)).reduce(add)
print('number of characters in file: %s' % chars)

# Get words from the input file
words =file_in.flatMap(lambda line: re.split('\W+', line.lower().
strip()))
# words of more than 3 characters
words = words.filter(lambda x: len(x) > 3)
# set count 1 per word
words = words.map(lambda w: (w,1))
# reduce phase - sum count all the words
words = words.reduceByKey(add)
```

In this program, we are first reading the file from the directory /home/an/ Documents/A00_Documents/Spark4Py 20150315 into file_in.

We are then introspecting the file by counting the number of lines and the number of characters per line.

We are splitting the input file in to words and getting them in lower case. For our word count purpose, we are choosing words longer than three characters in order to avoid shorter and much more frequent words such as *the, and, for* to skew the count in their favor. Generally, they are considered stop words and should be filtered out in any language processing task.

At this stage, we are getting ready for the MapReduce steps. To each word, we map a value of 1 and reduce it by summing all the unique words.

Here are illustrations of the code in the IPython Notebook. The first 10 cells are preprocessing the word count on the dataset, which is retrieved from the local file directory.

```
In [ ]:  # Pyspark context sc is up and running
         sc

In [1]:  # sc master - running locally
         sc.master

Out[1]:  u'local[*]'
```

Word count on manuscript using PySpark

```
In [3]:  # import regex module
         import re
         # import add from operator module
         from operator import add

In [4]:  # read input file
         file_in = sc.textFile('/home/an/Documents/A00_Documents/Spark4Py 20150315')

In [5]:  # count lines
         print('number of lines in file: %s' % file_in.count())
         #
         # add up lenths of each line
         chars = file_in.map(lambda s: len(s)).reduce(add)
         print('number of characters in file: %s' % chars)

         number of lines in file: 176
         number of characters in file: 11019

In [6]:  # Get words from the input file
         words =file_in.flatMap(lambda line: re.split('\W+', line.lower().strip()))

In [7]:  # words of more than 3 characters
         words = words.filter(lambda x: len(x) > 3)

In [8]:  # set count 1 per word
         words = words.map(lambda w: (w,1))

In [9]:  # reduce phase - sum count all the words
         words = words.reduceByKey(add)

In [10]: # create tuple (count, word) and sort in descending
         words = words.map(lambda x: (x[1], x[0])).sortByKey(False)
```

Swap the word count tuples in the format (count, word) in order to sort by count, which is now the primary key of the tuple:

```
# create tuple (count, word) and sort in descending
words = words.map(lambda x: (x[1], x[0])).sortByKey(False)

# take top 20 words by frequency
words.take(20)
```

In order to display our result, we are creating the tuple (count, word) and displaying the top 20 most frequently used words in descending order:

```
In [9]:  # reduce phase - sum count all the words
         words = words.reduceByKey(add)

In [10]: # create tuple (count, word) and sort in descending
         words = words.map(lambda x: (x[1], x[0])).sortByKey(False)

In [11]: # take top 20 words by frequency
         words.take(20)

Out[11]: [(45, u'spark'),
          (26, u'data'),
          (20, u'with'),
          (18, u'anaconda'),
          (16, u'layer'),
          (15, u'python'),
          (13, u'hadoop'),
          (12, u'such'),
          (11, u'from'),
          (11, u'install'),
          (10, u'distributed'),
          (10, u'will'),
          (9, u'processing'),
          (8, u'download'),
          (8, u'pyspark'),
          (8, u'cluster'),
          (7, u'environment'),
          (7, u'that'),
          (7, u'which'),
          (7, u'analytics')]

In [12]: # create function for histogram of most frequent words
         #

         % matplotlib inline
         import matplotlib.pyplot as plt
         #

         def histogram(words):
             count = map(lambda x: x[1], words)
             word = map(lambda x: x[0], words)
             plt.barh(range(len(count)), count,color = 'grey')
             plt.yticks(range(len(count)), word)

In [13]: # Change order of tuple (word, count) from (count, word)
         words = words.map(lambda x:(x[1], x[0]))
         words.take(25)
```

Let's create a histogram function:

```
# create function for histogram of most frequent words

% matplotlib inline
import matplotlib.pyplot as plt
#

def histogram(words):
    count = map(lambda x: x[1], words)
    word = map(lambda x: x[0], words)
    plt.barh(range(len(count)), count,color = 'grey')
    plt.yticks(range(len(count)), word)

# Change order of tuple (word, count) from (count, word)
words = words.map(lambda x:(x[1], x[0]))
words.take(25)

# display histogram
histogram(words.take(25))
```

Here, we visualize the most frequent words by plotting them in a bar chart. We have to first swap the tuple from the original (count, word) to (word, count):

```
In [13]:  # Change order of tuple (word, count) from (count, word)
          words = words.map(lambda x:(x[1], x[0]))
          words.take(25)
```

```
Out[13]:  [(u'spark', 45),
           (u'data', 26),
           (u'with', 20),
           (u'anaconda', 18),
           (u'layer', 16),
           (u'python', 15),
           (u'hadoop', 13),
           (u'such', 12),
           (u'from', 11),
           (u'install', 11),
           (u'distributed', 10),
           (u'will', 10),
           (u'processing', 9),
           (u'download', 8),
           (u'pyspark', 8),
           (u'cluster', 8),
           (u'environment', 7),
           (u'that', 7),
           (u'which', 7),
           (u'analytics', 7),
           (u'oracle', 7),
           (u'manager', 6),
           (u'large', 6),
           (u'following', 6),
           (u'machine', 6)]
```

```
In [14]:  # display histogram
          histogram(words.take(20))
```

So here you have it: the most frequent words used in the first chapter are **Spark**, followed by **Data** and **Anaconda**.

Virtualizing the environment with Vagrant

In order to create a portable Python and Spark environment that can be easily shared and cloned, the development environment can be built with a `vagrantfile`.

We will point to the **Massive Open Online Courses (MOOCs)** delivered by *Berkeley University and Databricks*:

- *Introduction to Big Data with Apache Spark, Professor Anthony D. Joseph* can be found at https://www.edx.org/course/introduction-big-data-apache-spark-uc-berkeleyx-cs100-1x

- *Scalable Machine Learning, Professor Ameet Talwalkar* can be found at https://www.edx.org/course/scalable-machine-learning-uc-berkeleyx-cs190-1x

The course labs were executed on IPython Notebooks powered by PySpark. They can be found in the following GitHub repository: https://github.com/spark-mooc/mooc-setup/.

Once you have set up Vagrant on your machine, follow these instructions to get started: https://docs.vagrantup.com/v2/getting-started/index.html.

Clone the `spark-mooc/mooc-setup/` `github` repository in your work directory and launch the command $ `vagrant up`, within the cloned directory:

Be aware that the version of Spark may be outdated as the `vagrantfile` may not be up-to-date.

You will see an output similar to this:

```
C:\Programs\spark\edx1001\mooc-setup-master>vagrant up
Bringing machine 'sparkvm' up with 'virtualbox' provider...
==> sparkvm: Checking if box 'sparkmooc/base' is up to date...
==> sparkvm: Clearing any previously set forwarded ports...
==> sparkvm: Clearing any previously set network interfaces...
==> sparkvm: Preparing network interfaces based on configuration...
    sparkvm: Adapter 1: nat
==> sparkvm: Forwarding ports...
    sparkvm: 8001 => 8001 (adapter 1)
    sparkvm: 4040 => 4040 (adapter 1)
    sparkvm: 22 => 2222 (adapter 1)
==> sparkvm: Booting VM...
==> sparkvm: Waiting for machine to boot. This may take a few minutes...
    sparkvm: SSH address: 127.0.0.1:2222
    sparkvm: SSH username: vagrant
    sparkvm: SSH auth method: private key
```

```
    sparkvm: Warning: Connection timeout. Retrying...
    sparkvm: Warning: Remote connection disconnect. Retrying...
==> sparkvm: Machine booted and ready!
==> sparkvm: Checking for guest additions in VM...
==> sparkvm: Setting hostname...
==> sparkvm: Mounting shared folders...
    sparkvm: /vagrant => C:/Programs/spark/edx1001/mooc-setup-master
==> sparkvm: Machine already provisioned. Run `vagrant provision` or use
the `--provision`
==> sparkvm: to force provisioning. Provisioners marked to run always
will still run.


C:\Programs\spark\edx1001\mooc-setup-master>
```

This will launch the IPython Notebooks powered by PySpark on `localhost:8001`:

Moving to the cloud

As we are dealing with distributed systems, an environment on a virtual machine running on a single laptop is limited for exploration and learning. We can move to the cloud in order to experience the power and scalability of the Spark distributed framework.

Deploying apps in Amazon Web Services

Once we are ready to scale our apps, we can migrate our development environment to **Amazon Web Services (AWS)**.

How to run Spark on EC2 is clearly described in the following page: `https://spark.apache.org/docs/latest/ec2-scripts.html`.

We emphasize five key steps in setting up the AWS Spark environment:

1. Create an AWS EC2 key pair via the AWS console `http://aws.amazon.com/console/`.

2. Export your key pair to your environment:
   ```
   export AWS_ACCESS_KEY_ID=accesskeyid
   export AWS_SECRET_ACCESS_KEY=secretaccesskey
   ```

3. Launch your cluster:
   ```
   ~$ cd $SPARK_HOME/ec2
   ec2$ ./spark-ec2 -k <keypair> -i <key-file> -s <num-slaves> launch <cluster-name>
   ```

4. SSH into a cluster to run Spark jobs:
   ```
   ec2$ ./spark-ec2 -k <keypair> -i <key-file> login <cluster-name>
   ```

5. Destroy your cluster after usage:
   ```
   ec2$ ./spark-ec2 destroy <cluster-name>
   ```

Virtualizing the environment with Docker

In order to create a portable Python and Spark environment that can be easily shared and cloned, the development environment can be built in Docker containers.

We wish capitalize on Docker's two main functions:

* Creating isolated containers that can be easily deployed on different operating systems or in the cloud.

- Allowing easy sharing of the development environment image with all its dependencies using The DockerHub. The DockerHub is similar to GitHub. It allows easy cloning and version control. The snapshot image of the configured environment can be the baseline for further enhancements.

The following diagram illustrates a Docker-enabled environment with Spark, Anaconda, and the database server and their respective data volumes.

Docker offers the ability to clone and deploy an environment from the Dockerfile.

You can find an example Dockerfile with a PySpark and Anaconda setup at the following address: `https://hub.docker.com/r/thisgokeboysef/pyspark-docker/~/dockerfile/`.

Install Docker as per the instructions provided at the following links:

- `http://docs.docker.com/mac/started/` if you are on Mac OS X
- `http://docs.docker.com/linux/started/` if you are on Linux
- `http://docs.docker.com/windows/started/` if you are on Windows

Install the docker container with the Dockerfile provided earlier with the following command:

```
$ docker pull thisgokeboysef/pyspark-docker
```

Other great sources of information on how to *dockerize* your environment can be seen at Lab41. The GitHub repository contains the necessary code:

`https://github.com/Lab41/ipython-spark-docker`

The supporting blog post is rich in information on thought processes involved in building the docker environment: `http://lab41.github.io/blog/2015/04/13/ipython-on-spark-on-docker/`.

Summary

We set the context of building data-intensive apps by describing the overall architecture structured around the infrastructure, persistence, integration, analytics, and engagement layers. We also discussed Spark and Anaconda with their respective building blocks. We set up an environment in a VirtualBox with Anaconda and Spark and demonstrated a word count app using the text content of the first chapter as input.

In the next chapter, we will delve more deeply into the architecture blueprint for data-intensive apps and tap into the Twitter, GitHub, and Meetup APIs to get a feel of the data we will be mining with Spark.

2
Building Batch and Streaming Apps with Spark

The objective of the book is to teach you about PySpark and the PyData libraries by building an app that analyzes the Spark community's interactions on social networks. We will gather information on Apache Spark from GitHub, check the relevant tweets on Twitter, and get a feel for the buzz around Spark in the broader open source software communities using **Meetup**.

In this chapter, we will outline the various sources of data and information. We will get an understanding of their structure. We will outline the data processing pipeline, from collection to batch and streaming processing.

In this section, we will cover the following points:

- Outline data processing pipelines from collection to batch and stream processing, effectively depicting the architecture of the app we are planning to build.

- Check out the various data sources (GitHub, Twitter, and Meetup), their data structure (JSON, structured information, unstructured text, geo-location, time series data, and so on), and their complexities. We also discuss the tools to connect to three different APIs, so you can build your own data mashups. The book will focus on Twitter in the following chapters.

Architecting data-intensive apps

We defined the data-intensive app framework architecture blueprint in the previous chapter. Let's put back in context the various software components we are going to use throughout the book in our original framework. Here's an illustration of the various components of software mapped in the data-intensive architecture framework:

Data Intensive App Framework			
Engagement Layer			
Bokeh *Visualization (Charts, Time Series, Maps...)*			
Analytics Layer			
Spark SQL - Blaze *Exploration*	Spark MLlib *Machine Learning*	Spark GraphX *Graph*	Spark Streaming *Streaming*
Integration Layer			
Blaze – SparkSQL - Pandas *Connect – Collect – Correct – Compose – Consume*			
Persistence Layer			
MySQL - PostgreSQL *RDBMS*	Redis -HDFS *K-V Store - File Systems*	MongoDB *Document DB*	Cassandra *Columnar DB*
Infrastructure Layer			
VirtualBox - Vagrant *Virtualization*	Amazon Web Services Anaconda Cluster *Scalability*	Docker/Chef/Puppet/Ansible *Continuous Integration*	

Spark is an extremely efficient, distributed computing framework. In order to exploit its full power, we need to architect our solution accordingly. For performance reasons, the overall solution needs to also be aware of its usage in terms of CPU, storage, and network.

These imperatives drive the architecture of our solution:

- **Latency**: This architecture combines slow and fast processing. Slow processing is done on historical data in batch mode. This is also called data at rest. This phase builds precomputed models and data patterns that will be used by the fast processing arm once live continuous data is fed into the system. Fast processing of data or real-time analysis of streaming data refers to data in motion. Data at rest is essentially processing data in batch mode with a longer latency. Data in motion refers to the streaming computation of data ingested in real time.

- **Scalability**: Spark is natively linearly scalable through its distributed in-memory computing framework. Databases and data stores interacting with Spark need to be also able to scale linearly as data volume grows.

- **Fault tolerance**: When a failure occurs due to hardware, software, or network reasons, the architecture should be resilient enough and provide availability at all times.

- **Flexibility**: The data pipelines put in place in this architecture can be adapted and retrofitted very quickly depending on the use case.

Spark is unique as it allows batch processing and streaming analytics on the same unified platform.

We will consider two data processing pipelines:

- The first one handles data at rest and is focused on putting together the pipeline for batch analysis of the data

- The second one, data in motion, targets real-time data ingestion and delivering insights based on precomputed models and data patterns

Processing data at rest

Let's get an understanding of the data at rest or batch processing pipeline. The objective in this pipeline is to ingest the various datasets from Twitter, GitHub, and Meetup; prepare the data for Spark MLlib, the machine learning engine; and derive the base models that will be applied for insight generation in batch mode or in real time.

The following diagram illustrates the data pipeline in order to enable processing data at rest:

Processing Data At Rest

Twitter	Preparation	Persist	Feature Engineering	Data Modelling	Data Visualization
REST API Streaming	*Data Exploration Schema Attributes*	*JSON CSV Pickle*	*Dimensionality Reduction Feature Selection*	*Supervised Learning Classification Regression*	*Charts Histograms*
Github *API*	*Sample Transform Aggregate Normalize Join NLP*	*MySQL MongoDB Cassandra*	*NLP Tokenizer TF-IDF*	*Unsupervised Learning Clustering Anomaly Detection Frequent Itemset*	*Time series Geolocation*
Meetup *API*				*Collaborative Filter*	

Processing data in motion

Processing data in motion introduces a new level of complexity, as we are introducing a new possibility of failure. If we want to scale, we need to consider bringing in distributed message queue systems such as Kafka. We will dedicate a subsequent chapter to understanding streaming analytics.

The following diagram depicts a data pipeline for processing data in motion:

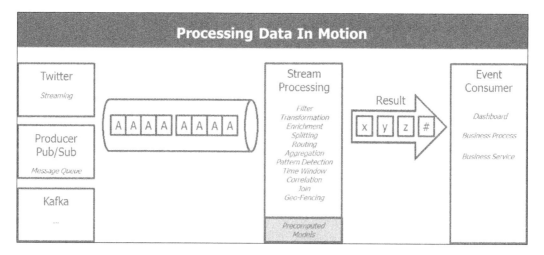

Exploring data interactively

Building a data-intensive app is not as straightforward as exposing a database to a web interface. During the setup of both the data at rest and data in motion processing, we will capitalize on Spark's ability to analyse data interactively and refine the data richness and quality required for the machine learning and streaming activities. Here, we will go through an iterative cycle of data collection, refinement, and investigation in order to get to the dataset of interest for our apps.

Connecting to social networks

Let's delve into the first steps of the data-intensive app architecture's integration layer. We are going to focus on harvesting the data, ensuring its integrity and preparing for batch and streaming data processing by Spark at the next stage. This phase is described in the five process steps: *connect*, *correct*, *collect*, *compose*, and *consume*. These are iterative steps of data exploration that will get us acquainted with the data and help us refine the data structure for further processing.

The following diagram depicts the iterative process of data acquisition and refinement for consumption:

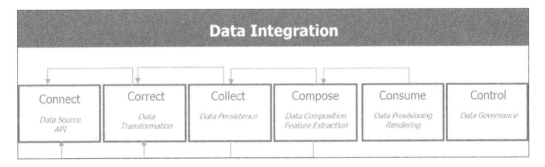

We connect to the social networks of interest: Twitter, GitHub, and Meetup. We will discuss the mode of access to the **APIs** (short for **Application Programming Interface**) and how to create a RESTful connection with those services while respecting the rate limitation imposed by the social networks. **REST** (short for **Representation State Transfer**) is the most widely adopted architectural style on the Internet in order to enable scalable web services. It relies on exchanging messages predominantly in **JSON** (short for **JavaScript Object Notation**). RESTful APIs and web services implement the four most prevalent verbs GET, PUT, POST, and DELETE. GET is used to retrieve an element or a collection from a given URI. PUT updates a collection with a new one. POST allows the creation of a new entry, while DELETE eliminates a collection.

Getting Twitter data

Twitter allows access to registered users to its search and streaming tweet services under an authorization protocol called OAuth that allows API applications to securely act on a user's behalf. In order to create the connection, the first step is to create an application with Twitter at `https://apps.twitter.com/app/new`.

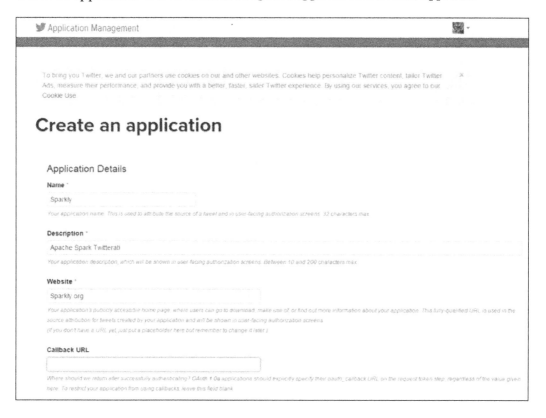

Once the application has been created, Twitter will issue the four codes that will allow it to tap into the Twitter hose:

```
CONSUMER_KEY = 'GetYourKey@Twitter'
CONSUMER_SECRET = ' GetYourKey@Twitter'
OAUTH_TOKEN = ' GetYourToken@Twitter'
OAUTH_TOKEN_SECRET = ' GetYourToken@Twitter'
```

If you wish to get a feel for the various RESTful queries offered, you can explore the Twitter API on the dev console at `https://dev.twitter.com/rest/tools/console`:

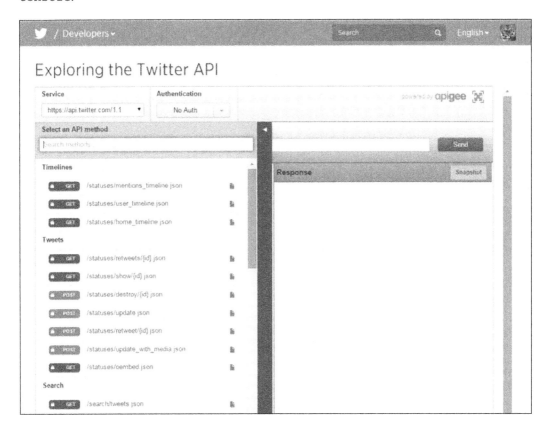

We will make a programmatic connection on Twitter using the following code, which will activate our OAuth access and allows us to tap into the Twitter API under the rate limitation. In the streaming mode, the limitation is for a GET request.

Getting GitHub data

GitHub uses a similar authentication process to Twitter. Head to the developer site and retrieve your credentials after duly registering with GitHub at `https://developer.github.com/v3/:`

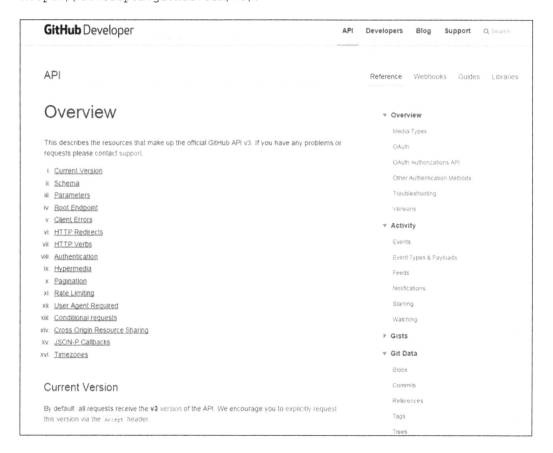

Getting Meetup data

Meetup can be accessed using the token issued in the developer resources to members of Meetup.com. The necessary token or OAuth credential for Meetup API access can be obtained on their developer's website at `https://secure.meetup.com/meetup_api:`

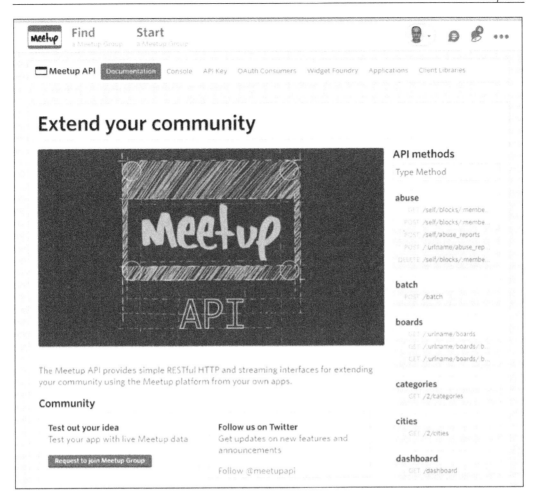

Analyzing the data

Let's get a first feel for the data extracted from each of the social networks and get an understanding of the data structure from each these sources.

Discovering the anatomy of tweets

In this section, we are going to establish connection with the Twitter API. Twitter offers two connection modes: the REST API, which allows us to search historical tweets for a given search term or hashtag, and the streaming API, which delivers real-time tweets under the rate limit in place.

In order to get a better understanding of how to operate with the Twitter API, we will go through the following steps:

1. Install the Twitter Python library.

2. Establish a connection programmatically via OAuth, the authentication required for Twitter.

3. Search for recent tweets for the query *Apache Spark* and explore the results obtained.

4. Decide on the key attributes of interest and retrieve the information from the JSON output.

Let's go through it step-by-step:

1. Install the Python Twitter library. In order to install it, you need to write `pip install twitter` from the command line:

   ```
   $ pip install twitter
   ```

2. Create the Python Twitter API class and its base methods for authentication, searching, and parsing the results. `self.auth` gets the credentials from Twitter. It then creates a registered API as `self.api`. We have implemented two methods: the first one to search Twitter with a given query and the second one to parse the output to retrieve relevant information such as the tweet ID, the tweet text, and the tweet author. The code is as follows:

   ```
   import twitter
   import urlparse
   from pprint import pprint as pp

   class TwitterAPI(object):
       """
       TwitterAPI class allows the Connection to Twitter via OAuth
       once you have registered with Twitter and receive the
       necessary credentiials
       """

   # initialize and get the twitter credentials
       def __init__(self):
           consumer_key = 'Provide your credentials'
           consumer_secret = 'Provide your credentials'
           access_token = 'Provide your credentials'
           access_secret = 'Provide your credentials'

           self.consumer_key = consumer_key
           self.consumer_secret = consumer_secret
   ```

```
        self.access_token = access_token
        self.access_secret = access_secret


#
# authenticate credentials with Twitter using OAuth
        self.auth = twitter.oauth.OAuth(access_token, access_
secret, consumer_key, consumer_secret)
    # creates registered Twitter API
        self.api = twitter.Twitter(auth=self.auth)
#
# search Twitter with query q (i.e. "ApacheSpark") and max. result
    def searchTwitter(self, q, max_res=10,**kwargs):
        search_results = self.api.search.tweets(q=q, count=10,
**kwargs)
        statuses = search_results['statuses']
        max_results = min(1000, max_res)


        for _ in range(10):
            try:
                next_results = search_results['search_metadata']
['next_results']
            except KeyError as e:
                break

            next_results = urlparse.parse_qsl(next_results[1:])
            kwargs = dict(next_results)
            search_results = self.api.search.tweets(**kwargs)
            statuses += search_results['statuses']

            if len(statuses) > max_results:
                break
        return statuses
#
# parse tweets as it is collected to extract id, creation
# date, user id, tweet text
    def parseTweets(self, statuses):
        return [ (status['id'],
                    status['created_at'],
                    status['user']['id'],
                    status['user']['name'],
                    status['text'], url['expanded_url'])
                        for status in statuses
                            for url in status['entities']['urls']
]
```

3. Instantiate the class with the required authentication:

```
t= TwitterAPI()
```

4. Run a search on the query term *Apache Spark*:

```
q="ApacheSpark"
tsearch = t.searchTwitter(q)
```

5. Analyze the JSON output:

```
pp(tsearch[1])

{u'contributors': None,
 u'coordinates': None,
 u'created_at': u'Sat Apr 25 14:50:57 +0000 2015',
 u'entities': {u'hashtags': [{u'indices': [74, 86], u'text':
u'sparksummit'}],
               u'media': [{u'display_url': u'pic.twitter.com/
WKUMRXxIWZ',
                           u'expanded_url': u'http://twitter.com/
bigdata/status/591976255831969792/photo/1',
                           u'id': 591976255156715520,
                           u'id_str': u'591976255156715520',
                           u'indices': [143, 144],
                           u'media_url':
...(snip)...
 u'text': u'RT @bigdata: Enjoyed catching up with @ApacheSpark
users &amp; leaders at #sparksummit NYC: video clips are out
http://t.co/qrqpP6cG9s http://t\u2026',
 u'truncated': False,
 u'user': {u'contributors_enabled': False,
           u'created_at': u'Sat Apr 04 14:44:31 +0000 2015',
           u'default_profile': True,
           u'default_profile_image': True,
           u'description': u'',
           u'entities': {u'description': {u'urls': []}},
           u'favourites_count': 0,
           u'follow_request_sent': False,
           u'followers_count': 586,
           u'following': False,
           u'friends_count': 2,
           u'geo_enabled': False,
           u'id': 3139047660,
           u'id_str': u'3139047660',
           u'is_translation_enabled': False,
           u'is_translator': False,
```

```
                     u'lang': u'zh-cn',
                     u'listed_count': 749,
                     u'location': u'',
                     u'name': u'Mega Data Mama',
                     u'notifications': False,
                     u'profile_background_color': u'C0DEED',
                     u'profile_background_image_url': u'http://abs.twimg.
com/images/themes/theme1/bg.png',
                     u'profile_background_image_url_https': u'https://abs.
twimg.com/images/themes/theme1/bg.png',
                     ...(snip)...
                     u'screen_name': u'MegaDataMama',
                     u'statuses_count': 26673,
                     u'time_zone': None,
                     u'url': None,
                     u'utc_offset': None,
                     u'verified': False}}
```

6. Parse the Twitter output to retrieve key information of interest:

```
tparsed = t.parseTweets(tsearch)
pp(tparsed)

[(591980327784046592,
  u'Sat Apr 25 15:01:23 +0000 2015',
  63407360,
  u'Jos\xe9 Carlos Baquero',
  u'Big Data systems are making a difference in the fight against
cancer. #BigData #ApacheSpark http://t.co/pnOLmsKdL9',
  u'http://tmblr.co/ZqTggs1jHytN0'),
 (591977704464875520,
  u'Sat Apr 25 14:50:57 +0000 2015',
  3139047660,
  u'Mega Data Mama',
  u'RT @bigdata: Enjoyed catching up with @ApacheSpark users &amp;
leaders at #sparksummit NYC: video clips are out http://t.co/
qrqpP6cG9s http://t\u2026',
  u'http://goo.gl/eF5xwK'),
 (591977172589539328,
  u'Sat Apr 25 14:48:51 +0000 2015',
  2997608763,
  u'Emma Clark',
  u'RT @bigdata: Enjoyed catching up with @ApacheSpark users &amp;
leaders at #sparksummit NYC: video clips are out http://t.co/
qrqpP6cG9s http://t\u2026',
  u'http://goo.gl/eF5xwK'),
```

```
... (snip)...
(591879098349268992,
 u'Sat Apr 25 08:19:08 +0000 2015',
 331263208,
 u'Mario Molina',
 u'#ApacheSpark speeds up big data decision-making http://t.
co/8hdEXreNfN',
 u'http://www.computerweekly.com/feature/Apache-Spark-speeds-up-
big-data-decision-making')]
```

Exploring the GitHub world

In order to get a better understanding on how to operate with the GitHub API, we will go through the following steps:

1. Install the GitHub Python library.

2. Access the API by using the token provided when we registered in the developer website.

3. Retrieve some key facts on the Apache foundation that is hosting the spark repository.

Let's go through the process step-by-step:

1. Install the Python PyGithub library. In order to install it, you need to `pip install PyGithub` from the command line:

   ```
   pip install PyGithub
   ```

2. Programmatically create a client to instantiate the GitHub API:

   ```
   from github import Github

   # Get your own access token

   ACCESS_TOKEN = 'Get_Your_Own_Access_Token'

   # We are focusing our attention to User = apache and Repo = spark

   USER = 'apache'
   REPO = 'spark'

   g = Github(ACCESS_TOKEN, per_page=100)
   user = g.get_user(USER)
   repo = user.get_repo(REPO)
   ```

3. Retrieve key facts from the Apache User. There are 640 active Apache repositories in GitHub:

```
repos_apache = [repo.name for repo in g.get_user('apache').get_
repos()]
len(repos_apache)
640
```

4. Retrieve key facts from the Spark repository, The programing languages used in the Spark repo are given here under:

```
pp(repo.get_languages())

{u'C': 1493,
 u'CSS': 4472,
 u'Groff': 5379,
 u'Java': 1054894,
 u'JavaScript': 21569,
 u'Makefile': 7771,
 u'Python': 1091048,
 u'R': 339201,
 u'Scala': 10249122,
 u'Shell': 172244}
```

5. Retrieve a few key participants of the wide Spark GitHub repository network. There are 3,738 stargazers in the Apache Spark repository at the time of writing. The network is immense. The first stargazer is *Matei Zaharia*, the cofounder of the Spark project when he was doing his PhD in Berkeley.

```
stargazers = [ s for s in repo.get_stargazers() ]
print "Number of stargazers", len(stargazers)
Number of stargazers 3738

[stargazers[i].login for i in range (0,20)]
[u'mateiz',
 u'beyang',
 u'abo',
 u'CodingCat',
 u'andy327',
 u'CrazyJvm',
 u'jyotiska',
 u'BaiGang',
 u'sundstei',
 u'dianacarroll',
 u'ybotco',
 u'xelax',
```

```
      u'prabeesh',
      u'invkrh',
      u'bedla',
      u'nadesai',
      u'pcpratts',
      u'narkisr',
      u'Honghe',
      u'Jacke']
```

Understanding the community through Meetup

In order to get a better understanding of how to operate with the Meetup API, we will go through the following steps:

1. Create a Python program to call the Meetup API using an authentication token.

2. Retrieve information of past events for meetup groups such as *London Data Science*.

3. Retrieve the profile of the meetup members in order to analyze their participation in similar meetup groups.

Let's go through the process step-by-step:

1. As there is no reliable Meetup API Python library, we will programmatically create a client to instantiate the Meetup API:

```
import json
import mimeparse
import requests
import urllib
from pprint import pprint as pp

MEETUP_API_HOST = 'https://api.meetup.com'
EVENTS_URL = MEETUP_API_HOST + '/2/events.json'
MEMBERS_URL = MEETUP_API_HOST + '/2/members.json'
GROUPS_URL = MEETUP_API_HOST + '/2/groups.json'
RSVPS_URL = MEETUP_API_HOST + '/2/rsvps.json'
PHOTOS_URL = MEETUP_API_HOST + '/2/photos.json'
GROUP_URLNAME = 'London-Machine-Learning-Meetup'
# GROUP_URLNAME = 'London-Machine-Learning-Meetup' # 'Data-
Science-London'
```

```
class Mee
tupAPI(object):
    """
    Retrieves information about meetup.com
    """
    def __init__(self, api_key, num_past_events=10, http_
timeout=1,
                 http_retries=2):
        """
        Create a new instance of MeetupAPI
        """
        self._api_key = api_key
        self._http_timeout = http_timeout
        self._http_retries = http_retries
        self._num_past_events = num_past_events

    def get_past_events(self):
        """
        Get past meetup events for a given meetup group
        """
        params = {'key': self._api_key,
                  'group_urlname': GROUP_URLNAME,
                  'status': 'past',
                  'desc': 'true'}
        if self._num_past_events:
            params['page'] = str(self._num_past_events)

        query = urllib.urlencode(params)
        url = '{0}?{1}'.format(EVENTS_URL, query)
        response = requests.get(url, timeout=self._http_timeout)
        data = response.json()['results']
        return data

    def get_members(self):
        """
        Get meetup members for a given meetup group
        """
        params = {'key': self._api_key,
                  'group_urlname': GROUP_URLNAME,
                  'offset': '0',
                  'format': 'json',
                  'page': '100',
                  'order': 'name'}
        query = urllib.urlencode(params)
```

```
        url = '{0}?{1}'.format(MEMBERS_URL, query)
        response = requests.get(url, timeout=self._http_timeout)
        data = response.json()['results']
        return data

    def get_groups_by_member(self, member_id='38680722'):
        """
        Get meetup groups for a given meetup member
        """
        params = {'key': self._api_key,
                  'member_id': member_id,
                  'offset': '0',
                  'format': 'json',
                  'page': '100',
                  'order': 'id'}
        query = urllib.urlencode(params)
        url = '{0}?{1}'.format(GROUPS_URL, query)
        response = requests.get(url, timeout=self._http_timeout)
        data = response.json()['results']
        return data
```

2. Then, we will retrieve past events from a given Meetup group:

```
m = MeetupAPI(api_key='Get_Your_Own_Key')
last_meetups = m.get_past_events()
pp(last_meetups[5])
```

```
{u'created': 1401809093000,
 u'description': u"<p>We are hosting a joint meetup between Spark
London and Machine Learning London. Given the excitement in the
machine learning community around Spark at the moment a joint
meetup is in order!</p> <p>Michael Armbrust from the Apache Spark
core team will be flying over from the States to give us a talk in
person.\xa0Thanks to our sponsors, Cloudera, MapR and Databricks
for helping make this happen.</p> <p>The first part of the talk
will be about MLlib, the machine learning library for Spark,\
xa0and the second part, on\xa0Spark SQL.</p> <p>Don't sign up if
you have already signed up on the Spark London page though!</p>
<p>\n\n\nAbstract for part one:</p> <p>In this talk, we\u20191l
introduce Spark and show how to use it to build fast, end-to-end
machine learning workflows. Using Spark\u2019s high-level API, we
can process raw data with familiar libraries in Java, Scala or
Python (e.g. NumPy) to extract the features for machine learning.
Then, using MLlib, its built-in machine learning library, we can
run scalable versions of popular algorithms. We\u20191l also cover
upcoming development work including new built-in algorithms and
R bindings.</p> <p>\n\n\n\nAbstract for part two:\xa0</p> <p>In
```

```
this talk, we'll examine Spark SQL, a new Alpha component that is
part of the Apache Spark 1.0 release. Spark SQL lets developers
natively query data stored in both existing RDDs and external
sources such as Apache Hive. A key feature of Spark SQL is the
ability to blur the lines between relational tables and RDDs,
making it easy for developers to intermix SQL commands that query
external data with complex analytics. In addition to Spark SQL,
we'll explore the Catalyst optimizer framework, which allows
Spark SQL to automatically rewrite query plans to execute more
efficiently.</p>",
 u'event_url': u'http://www.meetup.com/London-Machine-Learning-
Meetup/events/186883262/',
 u'group': {u'created': 1322826414000,
            u'group_lat': 51.52000045776367,
            u'group_lon': -0.18000000715255737,
            u'id': 2894492,
            u'join_mode': u'open',
            u'name': u'London Machine Learning Meetup',
            u'urlname': u'London-Machine-Learning-Meetup',
            u'who': u'Machine Learning Enthusiasts'},
 u'headcount': 0,
 u'id': u'186883262',
 u'maybe_rsvp_count': 0,
 u'name': u'Joint Spark London and Machine Learning Meetup',
 u'rating': {u'average': 4.800000190734863, u'count': 5},
 u'rsvp_limit': 70,
 u'status': u'past',
 u'time': 1403200800000,
 u'updated': 1403450844000,
 u'utc_offset': 3600000,
 u'venue': {u'address_1': u'12 Errol St, London',
            u'city': u'EC1Y 8LX',
            u'country': u'gb',
            u'id': 19504802,
            u'lat': 51.522533,
            u'lon': -0.090934,
            u'name': u'Royal Statistical Society',
            u'repinned': False},
 u'visibility': u'public',
 u'waitlist_count': 84,
 u'yes_rsvp_count': 70}
```

3. Get information about the Meetup members:

```
members = m.get_members()

{u'city': u'London',
  u'country': u'gb',
  u'hometown': u'London',
  u'id': 11337881,
  u'joined': 1421418896000,
  u'lat': 51.53,
  u'link': u'http://www.meetup.com/members/11337881',
  u'lon': -0.09,
  u'name': u'Abhishek Shivkumar',
  u'other_services': {u'twitter': {u'identifier': u'@
abhisemweb'}},
  u'photo': {u'highres_link': u'http://photos3.meetupstatic.com/
photos/member/9/6/f/3/highres_10898643.jpeg',
            u'photo_id': 10898643,
            u'photo_link': u'http://photos3.meetupstatic.com/
photos/member/9/6/f/3/member_10898643.jpeg',
            u'thumb_link': u'http://photos3.meetupstatic.com/
photos/member/9/6/f/3/thumb_10898643.jpeg'},
  u'self': {u'common': {}},
  u'state': u'17',
  u'status': u'active',
  u'topics': [{u'id': 1372, u'name': u'Semantic Web', u'urlkey':
u'semweb'},
            {u'id': 1512, u'name': u'XML', u'urlkey': u'xml'},
            {u'id': 49585,
             u'name': u'Semantic Social Networks',
             u'urlkey': u'semantic-social-networks'},
            {u'id': 24553,
             u'name': u'Natural Language Processing',
...(snip)...
             u'name': u'Android Development',
             u'urlkey': u'android-developers'}],
  u'visited': 1429281599000}
```

Previewing our app

Our challenge is to make sense of the data retrieved from these social networks, finding the key relationships and deriving insights. Some of the elements of interest are as follows:

- Visualizing the top influencers: Discover the top influencers in the community:
    ◦ Heavy Twitter users on *Apache Spark*
    ◦ Committers in GitHub
    ◦ Leading Meetup presentations

- Understanding the Network: Network graph of GitHub committers, watchers, and stargazers

- Identifying the Hot Locations: Locating the most active location for Spark

The following screenshot provides a preview of our app:

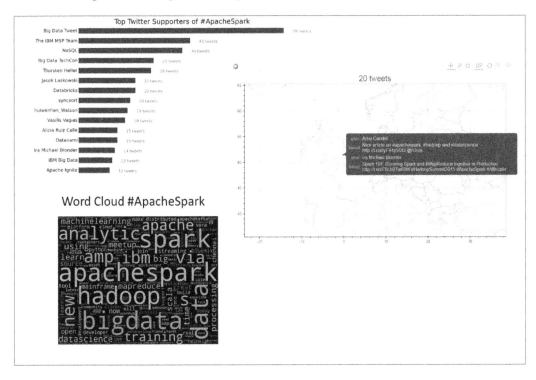

Summary

In this chapter, we laid out the overall architecture of our app. We explained the two main paradigms of processing data: batch processing, also called data at rest, and streaming analytics, referred to as data in motion. We proceeded to establish connections to three social networks of interest: Twitter, GitHub, and Meetup. We sampled the data and provided a preview of what we are aiming to build. The remainder of the book will focus on the Twitter dataset. We provided here the tools and API to access three social networks, so you can at a later stage create your own data mashups. We are now ready to investigate the data collected, which will be the topic of the next chapter.

In the next chapter, we will delve deeper into data analysis, extracting the key attributes of interest for our purposes and managing the storage of the information for batch and stream processing.

3
Juggling Data with Spark

As per the batch and streaming architecture laid out in the previous chapter, we need data to fuel our applications. We will harvest data focused on Apache Spark from Twitter. The objective of this chapter is to prepare data to be further used by the machine learning and streaming applications. This chapter focuses on how to exchange code and data across the distributed network. We will get practical insights into serialization, persistence, marshaling, and caching. We will get to grips with on Spark SQL, the key Spark module to interactively explore structured and semi-structured data. The fundamental data structure powering Spark SQL is the Spark dataframe. The Spark dataframe is inspired by the Python Pandas dataframe and the R dataframe. It is a powerful data structure, well understood and appreciated by data scientists with a background in R or Python.

In this chapter, we will cover the following points:

- Connect to Twitter, collect the relevant data, and then persist it in various formats such as JSON and CSV and data stores such as MongoDB

- Analyze the data using Blaze and Odo, a spin-off library from Blaze, in order to connect and transfer data from various sources and destinations

- Introduce Spark dataframes as the foundation for data interchange between the various Spark modules and explore data interactively using Spark SQL

Revisiting the data-intensive app architecture

Let's first put in context the focus of this chapter with respect to the data-intensive app architecture. We will concentrate our attention on the integration layer and essentially run through iterative cycles of the acquisition, refinement, and persistence of the data. This cycle was termed the five Cs. The five Cs stand for *connect, collect, correct, compose,* and *consume*. They are the essential processes we run through in the integration layer in order to get to the right quality and quantity of data retrieved from Twitter. We will also delve deeper in the persistence layer and set up a data store such as MongoDB to collect our data for processing later.

We will explore the data with Blaze, a Python library for data manipulation, and Spark SQL, the interactive module of Spark for data discovery powered by the Spark dataframe. The dataframe paradigm is shared by Python Pandas, Python Blaze, and Spark SQL. We will get a feel for the nuances of the three dataframe flavors.

The following diagram sets the context of the chapter's focus, highlighting the integration layer and the persistence layer:

Serializing and deserializing data

As we are harvesting data from web APIs under rate limit constraints, we need to store them. As the data is processed on a distributed cluster, we need consistent ways to save state and retrieve it for later usage.

Let's now define serialization, persistence, marshaling, and caching or memorization.

Serializing a Python object converts it into a stream of bytes. The Python object needs to be retrieved beyond the scope of its existence, when the program is shut. The serialized Python object can be transferred over a network or stored in a persistent storage. Deserialization is the opposite and converts the stream of bytes into the original Python object so the program can carry on from the saved state. The most popular serialization library in Python is Pickle. As a matter of fact, the PySpark commands are transferred over the wire to the worker nodes via pickled data.

Persistence saves a program's state data to disk or memory so that it can carry on where it left off upon restart. It saves a Python object from memory to a file or a database and loads it later with the same state.

Marshalling sends Python code or data over a network TCP connection in a multicore or distributed system.

Caching converts a Python object to a string in memory so that it can be used as a dictionary key later on. Spark supports pulling a dataset into a cluster-wide, in-memory cache. This is very useful when data is accessed repeatedly such as when querying a small reference dataset or running an iterative algorithm such as Google PageRank.

Caching is a crucial concept for Spark as it allows us to save RDDs in memory or with a spillage to disk. The caching strategy can be selected based on the lineage of the data or the **DAG** (short for **Directed Acyclic Graph**) of transformations applied to the RDDs in order to minimize shuffle or cross network heavy data exchange. In order to achieve good performance with Spark, beware of data shuffling. A good partitioning policy and use of RDD caching, coupled with avoiding unnecessary action operations, leads to better performance with Spark.

Harvesting and storing data

Before delving into database persistent storage such as MongoDB, we will look at some useful file storages that are widely used: **CSV** (short for **comma-separated values**) and **JSON** (short for **JavaScript Object Notation**) file storage. The enduring popularity of these two file formats lies in a few key reasons: they are human readable, simple, relatively lightweight, and easy to use.

Persisting data in CSV

The CSV format is lightweight, human readable, and easy to use. It has delimited text columns with an inherent tabular schema.

Python offers a robust `csv` library that can serialize a `csv` file into a Python dictionary. For the purpose of our program, we have written a `python` class that manages to persist data in CSV format and read from a given CSV.

Let's run through the code of the class `IO_csv` object. The `__init__` section of the class basically instantiates the file path, the filename, and the file suffix (in this case, `.csv`):

```
class IO_csv(object):

    def __init__(self, filepath, filename, filesuffix='csv'):
        self.filepath = filepath        # /path/to/file without the /'
at the end
        self.filename = filename        # FILE_NAME
        self.filesuffix = filesuffix
```

The `save` method of the class uses a Python named tuple and the header fields of the `csv` file in order to impart a schema while persisting the rows of the CSV. If the `csv` file already exists, it will be appended and not overwritten otherwise; it will be created:

```
    def save(self, data, NTname, fields):
        # NTname = Name of the NamedTuple
        # fields = header of CSV - list of the fields name
        NTuple = namedtuple(NTname, fields)

        if os.path.isfile('{0}/{1}.{2}'.format(self.filepath, self.
filename, self.filesuffix)):
            # Append existing file
            with open('{0}/{1}.{2}'.format(self.filepath, self.
filename, self.filesuffix), 'ab') as f:
                writer = csv.writer(f)
                # writer.writerow(fields) # fields = header of CSV
                writer.writerows([row for row in map(NTuple._make,
data)])
                # list comprehension using map on the NamedTuple._
make() iterable and the data file to be saved
                # Notice writer.writerows and not writer.writerow
(i.e. list of multiple rows sent to csv file
        else:
            # Create new file
```

```
            with open('{0}/{1}.{2}'.format(self.filepath, self.
filename, self.filesuffix), 'wb') as f:
                writer = csv.writer(f)
                writer.writerow(fields) # fields = header of CSV -
list of the fields name
                writer.writerows([row for row in map(NTuple._make,
data)])
                #  list comprehension using map on the NamedTuple._
make() iterable and the data file to be saved
                # Notice writer.writerows and not writer.writerow
(i.e. list of multiple rows sent to csv file
```

The `load` method of the class also uses a Python named tuple and the header fields of the `csv` file in order to retrieve the data using a consistent schema. The `load` method is a memory-efficient generator to avoid loading a huge file in memory: hence we use `yield` in place of `return`:

```
    def load(self, NTname, fields):
        # NTname = Name of the NamedTuple
        # fields = header of CSV - list of the fields name
        NTuple = namedtuple(NTname, fields)
        with open('{0}/{1}.{2}'.format(self.filepath, self.filename,
self.filesuffix),'rU') as f:
            reader = csv.reader(f)
            for row in map(NTuple._make, reader):
                # Using map on the NamedTuple._make() iterable and the
reader file to be loaded
                yield row
```

Here's the named tuple. We are using it to parse the tweet in order to save or retrieve them to and from the `csv` file:

```
fields01 = ['id', 'created_at', 'user_id', 'user_name', 'tweet_text',
'url']
Tweet01 = namedtuple('Tweet01',fields01)

def parse_tweet(data):
    """
    Parse a ``tweet`` from the given response data.
    """
    return Tweet01(
        id=data.get('id', None),
        created_at=data.get('created_at', None),
        user_id=data.get('user_id', None),
        user_name=data.get('user_name', None),
        tweet_text=data.get('tweet_text', None),
        url=data.get('url')
    )
```

Persisting data in JSON

JSON is one of the most popular data formats for Internet-based applications. All the APIs we are dealing with, Twitter, GitHub, and Meetup, deliver their data in JSON format. The JSON format is relatively lightweight compared to XML and human readable, and the schema is embedded in JSON. As opposed to the CSV format, where all records follow exactly the same tabular structure, JSON records can vary in their structure. JSON is semi-structured. A JSON record can be mapped into a Python dictionary of dictionaries.

Let's run through the code of the class IO_json object. The __init__ section of the class basically instantiates the file path, the filename, and the file suffix (in this case, .json):

```
class IO_json(object):
    def __init__(self, filepath, filename, filesuffix='json'):
        self.filepath = filepath        # /path/to/file without the /'
at the end
        self.filename = filename        # FILE_NAME
        self.filesuffix = filesuffix
        # self.file_io = os.path.join(dir_name, .'.join((base_
filename, filename_suffix)))
```

The save method of the class uses utf-8 encoding in order to ensure read and write compatibility of the data. If the JSON file already exists, it will be appended and not overwritten; otherwise it will be created:

```
    def save(self, data):
        if os.path.isfile('{0}/{1}.{2}'.format(self.filepath, self.
filename, self.filesuffix)):
            # Append existing file
            with io.open('{0}/{1}.{2}'.format(self.filepath, self.
filename, self.filesuffix), 'a', encoding='utf-8') as f:
                f.write(unicode(json.dumps(data, ensure_ascii=
False))) # In python 3, there is no "unicode" function
                # f.write(json.dumps(data, ensure_ascii= False)) #
create a \" escape char for " in the saved file
        else:
            # Create new file
            with io.open('{0}/{1}.{2}'.format(self.filepath, self.
filename, self.filesuffix), 'w', encoding='utf-8') as f:
                f.write(unicode(json.dumps(data, ensure_ascii=
False)))
                # f.write(json.dumps(data, ensure_ascii= False))
```

The `load` method of the class just returns the file that has been read. A further `json.loads` function needs to be applied in order to retrieve the `json` out of the file read:

```
    def load(self):
        with io.open('{0}/{1}.{2}'.format(self.filepath, self.
filename, self.filesuffix), encoding='utf-8') as f:
            return f.read()
```

Setting up MongoDB

It is crucial to store the information harvested. Thus, we set up MongoDB as our main document data store. As all the information collected is in JSON format and MongoDB stores information in **BSON** (short for **Binary JSON**), it is therefore a natural choice.

We will run through the following steps now:

- Installing the MongoDB server and client
- Running the MongoDB server
- Running the Mongo client
- Installing the PyMongo driver
- Creating the Python Mongo client

Installing the MongoDB server and client

In order to install the MongoDB package, perform through the following steps:

1. Import the public key used by the package management system (in our case, Ubuntu's `apt`). To import the MongoDB public key, we issue the following command:

   ```
   sudo apt-key adv --keyserver hkp://keyserver.ubuntu.com:80 --recv
   7F0CEB10
   ```

2. Create a list file for MongoDB. To create the list file, we use the following command:

   ```
   echo "deb http://repo.mongodb.org/apt/ubuntu "$("lsb_release
   -sc)"/ mongodb-org/3.0 multiverse" | sudo tee /etc/apt/sources.
   list.d/mongodb-org-3.0.list
   ```

3. Update the local package database as `sudo`:

   ```
   sudo apt-get update
   ```

4. Install the MongoDB packages. We install the latest stable version of MongoDB with the following command:

```
sudo apt-get install -y mongodb-org
```

Running the MongoDB server

Let's start the MongoDB server:

1. To start MongoDB server, we issue the following command to start mongod:

```
sudo service mongodb start
```

2. To check whether mongod has started properly, we issue the command:

```
an@an-VB:/usr/bin$ ps -ef | grep mongo
mongodb    967    1  4 07:03 ?        00:02:02 /usr/bin/mongod
--config /etc/mongod.conf
an        3143  3085  0 07:45 pts/3    00:00:00 grep --color=auto
mongo
```

In this case, we see that mongodb is running in process 967.

3. The mongod server sends a message to the effect that it is waiting for connection on port 27017. This is the default port for MongoDB. It can be changed in the configuration file.

4. We can check the contents of the log file at /var/log/mongod/mongod.log:

```
an@an-VB:/var/lib/mongodb$ ls -lru
total 81936
drwxr-xr-x 2 mongodb nogroup      4096 Apr 25 11:19 _tmp
-rw-r--r-- 1 mongodb nogroup        69 Apr 25 11:19 storage.bson
-rwxr-xr-x 1 mongodb nogroup         5 Apr 25 11:19 mongod.lock
-rw------- 1 mongodb nogroup 16777216 Apr 25 11:19 local.ns
-rw------- 1 mongodb nogroup 67108864 Apr 25 11:19 local.0
drwxr-xr-x 2 mongodb nogroup      4096 Apr 25 11:19 journal
```

5. In order to stop the mongodb server, just issue the following command:

```
sudo service mongodb stop
```

Running the Mongo client

Running the Mongo client in the console is as easy as calling mongo, as highlighted in the following command:

```
an@an-VB:/usr/bin$ mongo
MongoDB shell version: 3.0.2
connecting to: test
Server has startup warnings:
2015-05-30T07:03:49.387+0200 I CONTROL   [initandlisten]
2015-05-30T07:03:49.388+0200 I CONTROL   [initandlisten]
```

At the mongo client console prompt, we can see the databases with the following commands:

```
> show dbs
local  0.078GB
test   0.078GB
```

We select the test database using use test:

```
> use test
switched to db test
```

We display the collections within the test database:

```
> show collections
restaurants
system.indexes
```

We check a sample record in the restaurant collection listed previously:

```
> db.restaurants.find()
{ "_id" : ObjectId("553b70055e82e7b824ae0e6f"), "address : { "building
: "1007", "coord" : [ -73.856077, 40.848447 ], "street : "Morris Park
Ave", "zipcode : "10462 }, "borough" : "Bronx", "cuisine" : "Bakery",
"grades : [ { "grade : "A", "score" : 2, "date" : ISODate("2014-
03-03T00:00:00Z") }, { "date" : ISODate("2013-09-11T00:00:00Z"),
"grade : "A", "score" : 6 }, { "score" : 10, "date" : ISODate("2013-
01-24T00:00:00Z"), "grade" : "A }, { "date" : ISODate("2011-11-
23T00:00:00Z"), "grade : "A", "score" : 9 }, { "date" : ISODate("2011-
03-10T00:00:00Z"), "grade" : "B", "score" : 14 } ], "name : "Morris
Park Bake Shop", "restaurant_id : "30075445" }
```

Installing the PyMongo driver

Installing the Python driver with anaconda is easy. Just run the following command at the terminal:

```
conda install pymongo
```

Creating the Python client for MongoDB

We are creating a IO_mongo class that will be used in our harvesting and processing programs to store the data collected and retrieved saved information. In order to create the mongo client, we will import the MongoClient module from pymongo. We connect to the mongodb server on localhost at port 27017. The command is as follows:

```
from pymongo import MongoClient as MCli

class IO_mongo(object):
    conn={'host':'localhost', 'ip':'27017'}
```

We initialize our class with the client connection, the database (in this case, twtr_db), and the collection (in this case, twtr_coll) to be accessed:

```
def __init__(self, db='twtr_db', coll='twtr_coll', **conn ):
    # Connects to the MongoDB server
    self.client = MCli(**conn)
    self.db = self.client[db]
    self.coll = self.db[coll]
```

The save method inserts new records in the preinitialized collection and database:

```
def save(self, data):
    # Insert to collection in db
    return self.coll.insert(data)
```

The load method allows the retrieval of specific records according to criteria and projection. In the case of large amount of data, it returns a cursor:

```
def load(self, return_cursor=False, criteria=None,
projection=None):

        if criteria is None:
            criteria = {}

        if projection is None:
            cursor = self.coll.find(criteria)
        else:
```

```
        cursor = self.coll.find(criteria, projection)

    # Return a cursor for large amounts of data
    if return_cursor:
        return cursor
    else:
        return [ item for item in cursor ]
```

Harvesting data from Twitter

Each social network poses its limitations and challenges. One of the main obstacles for harvesting data is an imposed rate limit. While running repeated or long-running connections between rates limit pauses, we have to be careful to avoid collecting duplicate data.

We have redesigned our connection programs outlined in the previous chapter to take care of the rate limits.

In this `TwitterAPI` class that connects and collects the tweets according to the search query we specify, we have added the following:

- Logging capability using the Python logging library with the aim of collecting any errors or warning in the case of program failure
- Persistence capability using MongoDB, with the `IO_mongo` class exposed previously as well as JSON file using the `IO_json` class
- API rate limit and error management capability, so we can ensure more resilient calls to Twitter without getting barred for tapping into the firehose

Let's go through the steps:

1. We initialize by instantiating the Twitter API with our credentials:

```
class TwitterAPI(object):
    """
    TwitterAPI class allows the Connection to Twitter via OAuth
    once you have registered with Twitter and receive the
    necessary credentials
    """

    def __init__(self):
        consumer_key = 'get_your_credentials'
        consumer_secret = get your_credentials'
        access_token = 'get_your_credentials'
```

```
        access_secret = 'get your_credentials'
        self.consumer_key = consumer_key
        self.consumer_secret = consumer_secret
        self.access_token = access_token
        self.access_secret = access_secret
        self.retries = 3
        self.auth = twitter.oauth.OAuth(access_token, access_
secret, consumer_key, consumer_secret)
        self.api = twitter.Twitter(auth=self.auth)
```

2. We initialize the logger by providing the log level:
   - ° `logger.debug`(debug message)
   - ° `logger.info`(info message)
   - ° `logger.warn`(warn message)
   - ° `logger.error`(error message)
   - ° `logger.critical`(critical message)

3. We set the log path and the message format:

```
        # logger initialisation
        appName = 'twt150530'
        self.logger = logging.getLogger(appName)
        #self.logger.setLevel(logging.DEBUG)
        # create console handler and set level to debug
        logPath = '/home/an/spark/spark-1.3.0-bin-hadoop2.4/
examples/AN_Spark/data'
        fileName = appName
        fileHandler = logging.FileHandler("{0}/{1}.log".
format(logPath, fileName))
        formatter = logging.Formatter('%(asctime)s - %(name)s -
%(levelname)s - %(message)s')
        fileHandler.setFormatter(formatter)
        self.logger.addHandler(fileHandler)
        self.logger.setLevel(logging.DEBUG)
```

4. We initialize the JSON file persistence instruction:

```
        # Save to JSON file initialisation
        jsonFpath = '/home/an/spark/spark-1.3.0-bin-hadoop2.4/
examples/AN_Spark/data'
        jsonFname = 'twtr15053001'
        self.jsonSaver = IO_json(jsonFpath, jsonFname)
```

5. We initialize the MongoDB database and collection for persistence:

```
# Save to MongoDB Intitialisation
self.mongoSaver = IO_mongo(db='twtr01_db', coll='twtr01_
coll')
```

6. The method `searchTwitter` launches the search according to the query specified:

```
def searchTwitter(self, q, max_res=10,**kwargs):
    search_results = self.api.search.tweets(q=q, count=10,
**kwargs)
    statuses = search_results['statuses']
    max_results = min(1000, max_res)

    for _ in range(10):
        try:
            next_results = search_results['search_metadata']
['next_results']
            # self.logger.info('info' in searchTwitter - next_
results:%s'% next_results[1:])
        except KeyError as e:
            self.logger.error('error' in searchTwitter: %s',
%(e))
            break

        # next_results = urlparse.parse_qsl(next_results[1:])
# python 2.7
        next_results = urllib.parse.parse_qsl(next_
results[1:])
        # self.logger.info('info' in searchTwitter - next_
results[max_id]:', next_results[0:])
        kwargs = dict(next_results)
        # self.logger.info('info' in searchTwitter - next_
results[max_id]:%s'% kwargs['max_id'])
        search_results = self.api.search.tweets(**kwargs)
        statuses += search_results['statuses']
        self.saveTweets(search_results['statuses'])

        if len(statuses) > max_results:
            self.logger.info('info' in searchTwitter - got %i
tweets - max: %i' %(len(statuses), max_results))
            break
    return statuses
```

7. The `saveTweets` method actually saves the collected tweets in JSON and in MongoDB:

```
def saveTweets(self, statuses):
    # Saving to JSON File
    self.jsonSaver.save(statuses)

    # Saving to MongoDB
    for s in statuses:
        self.mongoSaver.save(s)
```

8. The `parseTweets` method allows us to extract the key tweet information from the vast amount of information provided by the Twitter API:

```
def parseTweets(self, statuses):
    return [ (status['id'],
              status['created_at'],
              status['user']['id'],
              status['user']['name']
              status['text''text'],
              url['expanded_url'])
                  for status in statuses
                      for url in status['entities']['urls']
]
```

9. The `getTweets` method calls the `searchTwitter` method described previously. The `getTweets` method ensures that API calls are made reliably whilst respecting the imposed rate limit. The code is as follows:

```
def getTweets(self, q,  max_res=10):
    """
    Make a Twitter API call whilst managing rate limit and
errors.
    """
    def handleError(e, wait_period=2, sleep_when_rate_
limited=True):
        if wait_period > 3600: # Seconds
            self.logger.error('Too many retries in getTweets:
%s', %(e))
            raise e
        if e.e.code == 401:
            self.logger.error('error 401 * Not Authorised * in
getTweets: %s', %(e))
            return None
        elif e.e.code == 404:
            self.logger.error('error 404 * Not Found * in
getTweets: %s', %(e))
```

```
                    return None
           elif e.e.code == 429:
               self.logger.error('error 429 * API Rate Limit
    Exceeded * in getTweets: %s', %(e))
               if sleep_when_rate_limited:
                   self.logger.error('error 429 * Retrying in 15
    minutes * in getTweets: %s', %(e))
                   sys.stderr.flush()
                   time.sleep(60*15 + 5)
                   self.logger.info('error 429 * Retrying now *
    in getTweets: %s', %(e))
                   return 2
               else:
                   raise e # Caller must handle the rate limiting
    issue
           elif e.e.code in (500, 502, 503, 504):
               self.logger.info('Encountered %i Error. Retrying
    in %i seconds' % (e.e.code, wait_period))
               time.sleep(wait_period)
               wait_period *= 1.5
               return wait_period
           else:
               self.logger.error('Exit - aborting - %s', %(e))
               raise e
```

10. Here, we are calling the `searchTwitter` API with the relevant query based on the parameters specified. If we encounter any error such as rate limitation from the provider, this will be processed by the `handleError` method:

```
    while True:
        try:
            self.searchTwitter( q, max_res=10)
        except twitter.api.TwitterHTTPError as e:
            error_count = 0
            wait_period = handleError(e, wait_period)
            if wait_period is None:
                return
```

Exploring data using Blaze

Blaze is an open source Python library, primarily developed by Continuum.io, leveraging Python Numpy arrays and Pandas dataframe. Blaze extends to out-of-core computing, while Pandas and Numpy are single-core.

Blaze offers an adaptable, unified, and consistent user interface across various backends. Blaze orchestrates the following:

- **Data**: Seamless exchange of data across storages such as CSV, JSON, HDF5, HDFS, and Bcolz files.

- **Computation**: Using the same query processing against computational backends such as Spark, MongoDB, Pandas, or SQL Alchemy.

- **Symbolic expressions**: Abstract expressions such as join, group-by, filter, selection, and projection with a syntax similar to Pandas but limited in scope. Implements the split-apply-combine methods pioneered by the R language.

Blaze expressions are lazily evaluated and in that respect share a similar processing paradigm with Spark RDDs transformations.

Let's dive into Blaze by first importing the necessary libraries: `numpy`, `pandas`, `blaze` and `odo`. Odo is a spin-off of Blaze and ensures data migration from various backends. The commands are as follows:

```
import numpy as np
import pandas as pd
from blaze import Data, by, join, merge
from odo import odo
BokehJS successfully loaded.
```

We create a Pandas `Dataframe` by reading the parsed tweets saved in a CSV file, `twts_csv`:

```
twts_pd_df = pd.DataFrame(twts_csv_read, columns=Tweet01._fields)
twts_pd_df.head()

Out[65]:
id    created_at    user_id    user_name    tweet_text    url
1    598831111406510082    2015-05-14 12:43:57    14755521
    raulsaeztapia    RT @pacoid: Great recap of @StrataConf EU˙ in L...
http://www.mango-solutions.com/wp/2015/05/the-...
2    598831111406510082    2015-05-14 12:43:57    14755521
    raulsaeztapia    RT @pacoid: Great recap of @StrataConf EU in L...
http://www.mango-solutions.com/wp/2015/05/the-...
3    98808944719593472    2015-05-14 11:15:52    14755521
    raulsaeztapia    RT @alvaroagea: Simply @ApacheSpark http://t.c...
http://www.webex.com/ciscospark/
4    598808944719593472    2015-05-14 11:15:52    14755521
    raulsaeztapia    RT @alvaroagea: Simply @ApacheSpark http://t.c...
http://sparkjava.com/
```

We run the Tweets Panda `Dataframe` to the `describe()` function to get some overall information on the dataset:

```
twts_pd_df.describe()
Out[66]:
id    created_at    user_id    user_name    tweet_text    url
count  19  19  19  19  19  19
unique    7  7  6  6    6  7
top    598808944719593472    2015-05-14 11:15:52    14755521
    raulsaeztapia    RT @alvaroagea: Simply @ApacheSpark http://t.c...
http://bit.ly/1HfdOXm
freq    6  6  9  9  6  6
```

We convert the Pandas `dataframe` into a Blaze `dataframe` by simply passing it through the `Data()` function:

```
#
# Blaze dataframe
#
twts_bz_df = Data(twts_pd_df)
```

We can retrieve the schema representation of the Blaze `dataframe` by passing the `schema` function:

```
twts_bz_df.schema
Out[73]:
dshape("""{
  id: ?string,
  created_at: ?string,
  user_id: ?string,
  user_name: ?string,
  tweet_text: ?string,
  url: ?string
  }""")
```

The `.dshape` function gives a record count and the schema:

```
twts_bz_df.dshape
Out[74]:
dshape("""19 * {
  id: ?string,
  created_at: ?string,
  user_id: ?string,
  user_name: ?string,
  tweet_text: ?string,
  url: ?string
  }""")
```

We can print the Blaze `dataframe` content:

```
twts_bz_df.data
Out[75]:
id     created_at    user_id    user_name    tweet_text    url
1     598831111406510082    2015-05-14 12:43:57    14755521
    raulsaeztapia    RT @pacoid: Great recap of @StrataConf EU in L...
http://www.mango-solutions.com/wp/2015/05/the-...
2     598831111406510082    2015-05-14 12:43:57    14755521
    raulsaeztapia    RT @pacoid: Great recap of @StrataConf EU in L...
http://www.mango-solutions.com/wp/2015/05/the-...
...
18     598782970082807808    2015-05-14 09:32:39    1377652806
    embeddedcomputer.nl    RT @BigDataTechCon: Moving Rating
Prediction w...    http://buff.ly/1QBpk8J
19     598777933730160640    2015-05-14 09:12:38    294862170    Ellen
Friedman    I'm still on Euro time. If you are too check o...
    http://bit.ly/1Hfd0Xm
```

We extract the column `tweet_text` and take the unique values:

```
twts_bz_df.tweet_text.distinct()
Out[76]:
    tweet_text
0    RT @pacoid: Great recap of @StrataConf EU in L...
1    RT @alvaroagea: Simply @ApacheSpark http://t.c...
2    RT @PrabhaGana: What exactly is @ApacheSpark a...
3    RT @Ellen_Friedman: I'm still on Euro time. If...
4    RT @BigDataTechCon: Moving Rating Prediction w...
5    I'm still on Euro time. If you are too check o...
```

We extract multiple columns `['id', 'user_name','tweet_text']` from the `dataframe` and take the unique records:

```
twts_bz_df[['id', 'user_name','tweet_text']].distinct()
Out[78]:
   id    user_name    tweet_text
0    598831111406510082    raulsaeztapia    RT @pacoid: Great recap of @
StrataConf EU in L...
1    598808944719593472    raulsaeztapia    RT @alvaroagea: Simply @
ApacheSpark http://t.c...
2    598796205091500032    John Humphreys    RT @PrabhaGana: What exactly
is @ApacheSpark a...
3    598788561127735296    Leonardo D'Ambrosi    RT @Ellen_Friedman: I'm
still on Euro time. If...
4    598785545557438464    Alexey Kosenkov    RT @Ellen_Friedman: I'm
still on Euro time. If...
```

```
5    598782970082807808    embedded computer.nl    RT @BigDataTechCon:
Moving Rating Prediction w...
6    598777933730160640    Ellen Friedman    I'm still on Euro time. If
you are too check o...
```

Transferring data using Odo

Odo is a spin-off project of Blaze. Odo allows the interchange of data. Odo ensures the migration of data across different formats (CSV, JSON, HDFS, and more) and across different databases (SQL databases, MongoDB, and so on) using a very simple predicate:

```
Odo(source, target)
```

To transfer to a database, the address is specified using a URL. For example, for a MongoDB database, it would look like this:

```
mongodb://username:password@hostname:port/database_name::collection_
name
```

Let's run some examples of using Odo. Here, we illustrate `odo` by reading a CSV file and creating a Blaze `dataframe`:

```
filepath   = csvFpath
filename   = csvFname
filesuffix = csvSuffix
twts_odo_df = Data('{0}/{1}.{2}'.format(filepath, filename,
filesuffix))
```

Count the number of records in the `dataframe`:

```
twts_odo_df.count()
Out[81]:
19
```

Display the five initial records of the `dataframe`:

```
twts_odo_df.head(5)
Out[82]:
  id    created_at    user_id    user_name    tweet_text    url
0    598831111406510082    2015-05-14 12:43:57    14755521
raulsaeztapia    RT @pacoid: Great recap of @StrataConf EU in L...
http://www.mango-solutions.com/wp/2015/05/the-...
1    598831111406510082    2015-05-14 12:43:57    14755521
raulsaeztapia    RT @pacoid: Great recap of @StrataConf EU in L...
http://www.mango-solutions.com/wp/2015/05/the-...
2    598808944719593472    2015-05-14 11:15:52    14755521
raulsaeztapia    RT @alvaroagea: Simply @ApacheSpark http://t.c...
```

```
http://www.webex.com/ciscospark/
3    598808944719593472    2015-05-14 11:15:52    14755521
raulsaeztapia    RT @alvaroagea: Simply @ApacheSpark http://t.c...
http://sparkjava.com/
4    598808944719593472    2015-05-14 11:15:52    14755521
raulsaeztapia    RT @alvaroagea: Simply @ApacheSpark http://t.c...
https://www.sparkfun.com/
```

Get `dshape` information from the `dataframe`, which gives us the number of records and the schema:

```
twts_odo_df.dshape
Out[83]:
dshape("var * {
  id: int64,
  created_at: ?datetime,
  user_id: int64,
  user_name: ?string,
  tweet_text: ?string,
  url: ?string
  }""")
```

Save a processed Blaze `dataframe` into JSON:

```
odo(twts_odo_distinct_df, '{0}/{1}.{2}'.format(jsonFpath, jsonFname,
jsonSuffix))
Out[92]:
<odo.backends.json.JSONLines at 0x7f77f0abfc50>
```

Convert a JSON file to a CSV file:

```
odo('{0}/{1}.{2}'.format(jsonFpath, jsonFname, jsonSuffix), '{0}/{1}.
{2}'.format(csvFpath, csvFname, csvSuffix))
Out[94]:
<odo.backends.csv.CSV at 0x7f77f0abfe10>
```

Exploring data using Spark SQL

Spark SQL is a relational query engine built on top of Spark Core. Spark SQL uses a query optimizer called **Catalyst**.

Relational queries can be expressed using SQL or HiveQL and executed against JSON, CSV, and various databases. Spark SQL gives us the full expressiveness of declarative programing with Spark dataframes on top of functional programming with RDDs.

Understanding Spark dataframes

Here's a tweet from @bigdata announcing Spark 1.3.0, the advent of Spark SQL and dataframes. It also highlights the various data sources in the lower part of the diagram. On the top part, we can notice R as the new language that will be gradually supported on top of Scala, Java, and Python. Ultimately, the Data Frame philosophy is pervasive between R, Python, and Spark.

Spark dataframes originate from SchemaRDDs. It combines RDD with a schema that can be inferred by Spark, if requested, when registering the dataframe. It allows us to query complex nested JSON data with plain SQL. Lazy evaluation, lineage, partitioning, and persistence apply to dataframes.

Let's query the data with Spark SQL, by first importing `SparkContext` and `SQLContext`:

```
from pyspark import SparkConf, SparkContext
from pyspark.sql import SQLContext, Row
In [95]:
sc
Out[95]:
<pyspark.context.SparkContext at 0x7f7829581890>
In [96]:
sc.master
Out[96]:
u'local[*]'
''In [98]:
# Instantiate Spark  SQL context
sqlc =  SQLContext(sc)
```

We read in the JSON file we saved with Odo:

```
twts_sql_df_01 = sqlc.jsonFile ("/home/an/spark/spark-1.3.0-bin-
hadoop2.4/examples/AN_Spark/data/twtr15051401_distinct.json")
In [101]:
twts_sql_df_01.show()
created_at            id                   tweet_text          user_id
user_name
2015-05-14T12:43:57Z 598831111406510082 RT @pacoid: Great... 14755521
raulsaeztapia
2015-05-14T11:15:52Z 598808944719593472 RT @alvaroagea: S... 14755521
raulsaeztapia
2015-05-14T10:25:15Z 598796205091500032 RT @PrabhaGana: W... 48695135
John Humphreys
2015-05-14T09:54:52Z 598788561127735296 RT @Ellen_Friedma...
2385931712 Leonardo D'Ambrosi
2015-05-14T09:42:53Z 598785545557438464 RT @Ellen_Friedma... 461020977
Alexey Kosenkov
2015-05-14T09:32:39Z 598782970082807808 RT @BigDataTechCo...
1377652806 embeddedcomputer.nl
2015-05-14T09:12:38Z 598777933730160640 I'm still on Euro... 294862170
Ellen Friedman
```

We print the schema of the Spark dataframe:

```
twts_sql_df_01.printSchema()
root
 |-- created_at: string (nullable = true)
 |-- id: long (nullable = true)
```

```
|-- tweet_text: string (nullable = true)
|-- user_id: long (nullable = true)
|-- user_name: string (nullable = true)
```

We select the `user_name` column from the dataframe:

```
twts_sql_df_01.select('user_name').show()
user_name
raulsaeztapia
raulsaeztapia
John Humphreys
Leonardo D'Ambrosi
Alexey Kosenkov
embeddedcomputer.nl
Ellen Friedman
```

We register the dataframe as a table, so we can execute a SQL query on it:

```
twts_sql_df_01.registerAsTable('tweets_01')
```

We execute a SQL statement against the dataframe:

```
twts_sql_df_01_selection = sqlc.sql("SELECT * FROM tweets_01 WHERE
user_name = 'raulsaeztapia'")
In [109]:
twts_sql_df_01_selection.show()
created_at              id                      tweet_text            user_id
user_name
2015-05-14T12:43:57Z 598831111406510082 RT @pacoid: Great... 14755521
raulsaeztapia
2015-05-14T11:15:52Z 598808944719593472 RT @alvaroagea: S... 14755521
raulsaeztapia
```

Let's process some more complex JSON; we read the original Twitter JSON file:

```
tweets_sqlc_inf = sqlc.jsonFile(infile)
```

Spark SQL is able to infer the schema of a complex nested JSON file:

```
tweets_sqlc_inf.printSchema()
root
 |-- contributors: string (nullable = true)
 |-- coordinates: string (nullable = true)
 |-- created_at: string (nullable = true)
 |-- entities: struct (nullable = true)
 |    |-- hashtags: array (nullable = true)
 |    |    |-- element: struct (containsNull = true)
```

```
|       |       |       |-- indices: array (nullable = true)
|       |       |       |    |-- element: long (containsNull = true)
|       |       |       |-- text: string (nullable = true)
|       |-- media: array (nullable = true)
|       |       |-- element: struct (containsNull = true)
|       |       |       |-- display_url: string (nullable = true)
|       |       |       |-- expanded_url: string (nullable = true)
|       |       |       |-- id: long (nullable = true)
|       |       |       |-- id_str: string (nullable = true)
|       |       |       |-- indices: array (nullable = true)
... (snip) ...
|       |-- statuses_count: long (nullable = true)
|       |-- time_zone: string (nullable = true)
|       |-- url: string (nullable = true)
|       |-- utc_offset: long (nullable = true)
|       |-- verified: boolean (nullable = true)
```

We extract the key information of interest from the wall of data by selecting specific columns in the dataframe (in this case, `['created_at', 'id', 'text', 'user.id', 'user.name', 'entities.urls.expanded_url']`):

```
tweets_extract_sqlc = tweets_sqlc_inf[['created_at', 'id', 'text',
'user.id', 'user.name', 'entities.urls.expanded_url']].distinct()
In [145]:
tweets_extract_sqlc.show()
created_at            id                  text                id
name                 expanded_url
Thu May 14 09:32:... 598782970082807808 RT @BigDataTechCo...
1377652806 embeddedcomputer.nl ArrayBuffer(http:...
Thu May 14 12:43:... 598831111406510082 RT @pacoid: Great... 14755521
raulsaeztapia        ArrayBuffer(http:...
Thu May 14 12:18:... 598824733086523393 @rabbitonweb spea...

...

Thu May 14 12:28:... 598827171168264192 RT @baandrzejczak... 20909005
Paweł Szulc          ArrayBuffer()
```

Understanding the Spark SQL query optimizer

We execute a SQL statement against the dataframe:

```
tweets_extract_sqlc_sel = sqlc.sql("SELECT * from Tweets_xtr_001 WHERE
name='raulsaeztapia'")
```

We get a detailed view of the query plans executed by Spark SQL:

- Parsed logical plan
- Analyzed logical plan
- Optimized logical plan
- Physical plan

The query plan uses Spark SQL's Catalyst optimizer. In order to generate the compiled bytecode from the query parts, the Catalyst optimizer runs through logical plan parsing and optimization followed by physical plan evaluation and optimization based on cost.

This is illustrated in the following tweet:

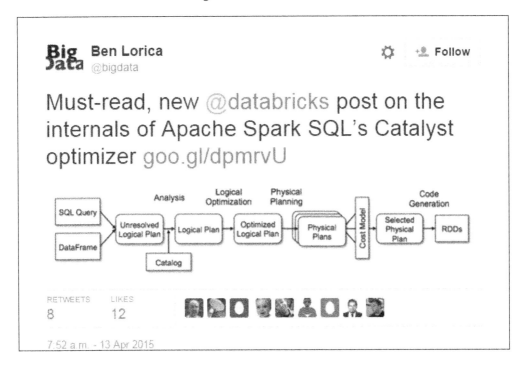

Looking back at our code, we call the .explain function on the Spark SQL query we just executed, and it delivers the full details of the steps taken by the Catalyst optimizer in order to assess and optimize the logical plan and the physical plan and get to the result RDD:

```
tweets_extract_sqlc_sel.explain(extended = True)
== Parsed Logical Plan ==
'Project [*]
 'Filter ('name = raulsaeztapia)'name'  'UnresolvedRelation' [Tweets_
xtr_001], None
== Analyzed Logical Plan ==
Project [created_at#7,id#12L,text#27,id#80L,name#81,expanded_url#82]
 Filter (name#81 = raulsaeztapia)
  Distinct
    Project [created_at#7,id#12L,text#27,user#29.id AS id#80L,user#29.
name AS name#81,entities#8.urls.expanded_url AS expanded_url#82]
     Relation[contributors#5,coordinates#6,created_
at#7,entities#8,favorite_count#9L,favorited#10,geo#11,id#12L,id_
str#13,in_reply_to_screen_name#14,in_reply_to_status_id#15,in_reply_
to_status_id_str#16,in_reply_to_user_id#17L,in_reply_to_user_id_str#
18,lang#19,metadata#20,place#21,possibly_sensitive#22,retweet_count#2
3L,retweeted#24,retweeted_status#25,source#26,text#27,truncated#28,us
er#29] JSONRelation(/home/an/spark/spark-1.3.0-bin-hadoop2.4/examples/
AN_Spark/data/twtr15051401.json,1.0,None)
== Optimized Logical Plan ==
Filter (name#81 = raulsaeztapia)
 Distinct
  Project [created_at#7,id#12L,text#27,user#29.id AS id#80L,user#29.
name AS name#81,entities#8.urls.expanded_url AS expanded_url#82]
    Relation[contributors#5,coordinates#6,created_
at#7,entities#8,favorite_count#9L,favorited#10,geo#11,id#12L,id_
str#13,in_reply_to_screen_name#14,in_reply_to_status_id#15,in_reply_
to_status_id_str#16,in_reply_to_user_id#17L,in_reply_to_user_id_str#
18,lang#19,metadata#20,place#21,possibly_sensitive#22,retweet_count#2
3L,retweeted#24,retweeted_status#25,source#26,text#27,truncated#28,us
er#29] JSONRelation(/home/an/spark/spark-1.3.0-bin-hadoop2.4/examples/
AN_Spark/data/twtr15051401.json,1.0,None)
== Physical Plan ==
Filter (name#81 = raulsaeztapia)
 Distinct false
  Exchange (HashPartitioning [created_at#7,id#12L,text#27,id#80L,name#
81,expanded_url#82], 200)
    Distinct true
     Project [created_at#7,id#12L,text#27,user#29.id AS id#80L,user#29.
name AS name#81,entities#8.urls.expanded_url AS expanded_url#82]
      PhysicalRDD [contributors#5,coordinates#6,created_
at#7,entities#8,favorite_count#9L,favorited#10,geo#11,id#12L,id_
```

```
str#13,in_reply_to_screen_name#14,in_reply_to_status_id#15,in_reply_
to_status_id_str#16,in_reply_to_user_id#17L,in_reply_to_user_id_str#
18,lang#19,metadata#20,place#21,possibly_sensitive#22,retweet_count#2
3L,retweeted#24,retweeted_status#25,source#26,text#27,truncated#28,us
er#29], MapPartitionsRDD[165] at map at JsonRDD.scala:41
Code Generation: false
== RDD ==
```

Finally, here's the result of the query:

```
tweets_extract_sqlc_sel.show()
created_at          id                      text                    id
name          expanded_url
Thu May 14 12:43:... 598831111406510082 RT @pacoid: Great... 14755521
raulsaeztapia ArrayBuffer(http:...
Thu May 14 11:15:... 598808944719593472 RT @alvaroagea: S... 14755521
raulsaeztapia ArrayBuffer(http:...
In [148]:
```

Loading and processing CSV files with Spark SQL

We will use the Spark package `spark-csv_2.11:1.2.0`. The command to be used to launch PySpark with the IPython Notebook and the `spark-csv` package should explicitly state the `–packages` argument:

`$ IPYTHON_OPTS='notebook' /home/an/spark/spark-1.5.0-bin-hadoop2.6/bin/`
`pyspark --packages com.databricks:spark-csv_2.11:1.2.0`

This will trigger the following output; we can see that the `spark-csv` package is installed with all its dependencies:

`an@an-VB:~/spark/spark-1.5.0-bin-hadoop2.6/examples/AN_Spark$ IPYTHON_`
`OPTS='notebook' /home/an/spark/spark-1.5.0-bin-hadoop2.6/bin/pyspark`
`--packages com.databricks:spark-csv_2.11:1.2.0`

```
... (snip) ...
Ivy Default Cache set to: /home/an/.ivy2/cache
The jars for the packages stored in: /home/an/.ivy2/jars
:: loading settings :: url = jar:file:/home/an/spark/spark-1.5.0-bin-
hadoop2.6/lib/spark-assembly-1.5.0-hadoop2.6.0.jar!/org/apache/ivy/
core/settings/ivysettings.xml
com.databricks#spark-csv_2.11 added as a dependency
:: resolving dependencies :: org.apache.spark#spark-submit-parent;1.0
  confs: [default]
  found com.databricks#spark-csv_2.11;1.2.0 in central
  found org.apache.commons#commons-csv;1.1 in central
```

```
    found com.univocity#univocity-parsers;1.5.1 in central
:: resolution report :: resolve 835ms :: artifacts dl 48ms
   :: modules in use:
   com.databricks#spark-csv_2.11;1.2.0 from central in [default]
   com.univocity#univocity-parsers;1.5.1 from central in [default]
   org.apache.commons#commons-csv;1.1 from central in [default]
   ---------------------------------------------------------------
   |                  |            modules       ||   artifacts   |
   |      conf        | number| search|dwnlded|evicted|| number|dwnlded|
   ---------------------------------------------------------------
   |     default      |   3   |   0   |   0   |   0   ||   3   |   0   |
   ---------------------------------------------------------------
:: retrieving :: org.apache.spark#spark-submit-parent
   confs: [default]
   0 artifacts copied, 3 already retrieved (0kB/45ms)
```

We are now ready to load our csv file and process it. Let's first import the
SQLContext:

```
#
# Read csv in a Spark DF
#
sqlContext = SQLContext(sc)
spdf_in = sqlContext.read.format('com.databricks.spark.csv')\
                                 .options(delimiter=";").
options(header="true")\
                                 .options(header='true').load(csv_
in)
```

We access the schema of the dataframe created from the loaded csv:

```
In [10]:
spdf_in.printSchema()
root
 |-- : string (nullable = true)
 |-- id: string (nullable = true)
 |-- created_at: string (nullable = true)
 |-- user_id: string (nullable = true)
 |-- user_name: string (nullable = true)
 |-- tweet_text: string (nullable = true)
```

We check the columns of the dataframe:

```
In [12]:
spdf_in.columns
Out[12]:
['', 'id', 'created_at', 'user_id', 'user_name', 'tweet_text']
```

We introspect the dataframe content:

```
In [13]:
spdf_in.show()
+---+-----------------+--------------------+----------+--------------
----+--------------------+
|   |               id|          created_at|   user_id|          user_
name|          tweet_text|
+---+-----------------+--------------------+----------+--------------
----+--------------------+
|  0|638830426971181057|Tue Sep 01 21:46:...|3276255125|          True
Equality|ernestsgantt: Bey...|
|  1|638830426727911424|Tue Sep 01 21:46:...|3276255125|          True
Equality|ernestsgantt: Bey...|
|  2|638830425402556417|Tue Sep 01 21:46:...|3276255125|          True
Equality|ernestsgantt: Bey...|
... (snip) ...
| 41|638830280988426250|Tue Sep 01 21:46:...| 951081582|          Jack
Baldwin|RT @cloudaus: We ...|
| 42|638830276626399232|Tue Sep 01 21:46:...|   6525302|Masayoshi
Nakamura|PynamoDB⬛⬛⬛⬛⬛⬛   |
+---+-----------------+--------------------+----------+--------------
----+--------------------+
only showing top 20 rows
```

Querying MongoDB from Spark SQL

There are two major ways to interact with MongoDB from Spark: the first is through the Hadoop MongoDB connector, and the second one is directly from Spark to MongoDB.

The first approach to interact with MongoDB from Spark is to set up a Hadoop environment and query through the Hadoop MongoDB connector. The connector details are hosted on GitHub at `https://github.com/mongodb/mongo-hadoop/wiki/Spark-Usage`. An actual use case is described in the series of blog posts from MongoDB:

- *Using MongoDB with Hadoop & Spark: Part 1 - Introduction & Setup* (`https://www.mongodb.com/blog/post/using-mongodb-hadoop-spark-part-1-introduction-setup`)

- *Using MongoDB with Hadoop and Spark: Part 2 - Hive Example* (`https://www.mongodb.com/blog/post/using-mongodb-hadoop-spark-part-2-hive-example`)

- *Using MongoDB with Hadoop & Spark: Part 3 - Spark Example & Key Takeaways* (`https://www.mongodb.com/blog/post/using-mongodb-hadoop-spark-part-3-spark-example-key-takeaways`)

Setting up a full Hadoop environment is bit elaborate. We will favor the second approach. We will use the `spark-mongodb` connector developed and maintained by Stratio. We are using the `Stratio spark-mongodb` package hosted at `spark.packages.org`. The packages information and version can be found in `spark.packages.org`:

> **Releases**
>
> Version: 0.10.1 (8263c8 | zip | jar) / Date: 2015-11-18 / License: Apache-2.0 / Scala version: 2.10
>
> (`http://spark-packages.org/package/Stratio/spark-mongodb`)

The command to launch PySpark with the IPython Notebook and the `spark-mongodb` package should explicitly state the packages argument:

```
$ IPYTHON_OPTS='notebook' /home/an/spark/spark-1.5.0-bin-hadoop2.6/bin/
pyspark --packages com.stratio.datasource:spark-mongodb_2.10:0.10.1
```

This will trigger the following output; we can see that the `spark-mongodb` package is installed with all its dependencies:

```
an@an-VB:~/spark/spark-1.5.0-bin-hadoop2.6/examples/AN_Spark$ IPYTHON_
OPTS='notebook' /home/an/spark/spark-1.5.0-bin-hadoop2.6/bin/pyspark
--packages com.stratio.datasource:spark-mongodb_2.10:0.10.1
... (snip) ...
Ivy Default Cache set to: /home/an/.ivy2/cache
The jars for the packages stored in: /home/an/.ivy2/jars
:: loading settings :: url = jar:file:/home/an/spark/spark-1.5.0-bin-
hadoop2.6/lib/spark-assembly-1.5.0-hadoop2.6.0.jar!/org/apache/ivy/
core/settings/ivysettings.xml
com.stratio.datasource#spark-mongodb_2.10 added as a dependency
:: resolving dependencies :: org.apache.spark#spark-submit-parent;1.0
  confs: [default]
  found com.stratio.datasource#spark-mongodb_2.10;0.10.1 in central
[W 22:10:50.910 NotebookApp] Timeout waiting for kernel_info reply
from 764081d3-baf9-4978-ad89-7735e6323cb6
  found org.mongodb#casbah-commons_2.10;2.8.0 in central
  found com.github.nscala-time#nscala-time_2.10;1.0.0 in central
  found joda-time#joda-time;2.3 in central
  found org.joda#joda-convert;1.2 in central
  found org.slf4j#slf4j-api;1.6.0 in central
  found org.mongodb#mongo-java-driver;2.13.0 in central
  found org.mongodb#casbah-query_2.10;2.8.0 in central
  found org.mongodb#casbah-core_2.10;2.8.0 in central
downloading https://repo1.maven.org/maven2/com/stratio/datasource/
spark-mongodb_2.10/0.10.1/spark-mongodb_2.10-0.10.1.jar ...
```

```
    [SUCCESSFUL ] com.stratio.datasource#spark-
mongodb_2.10;0.10.1!spark-mongodb_2.10.jar (3130ms)
downloading https://repo1.maven.org/maven2/org/mongodb/casbah-
commons_2.10/2.8.0/casbah-commons_2.10-2.8.0.jar ...
    [SUCCESSFUL ] org.mongodb#casbah-commons_2.10;2.8.0!casbah-
commons_2.10.jar (2812ms)
downloading https://repo1.maven.org/maven2/org/mongodb/casbah-
query_2.10/2.8.0/casbah-query_2.10-2.8.0.jar ...
    [SUCCESSFUL ] org.mongodb#casbah-query_2.10;2.8.0!casbah-query_2.10.
jar (1432ms)
downloading https://repo1.maven.org/maven2/org/mongodb/casbah-
core_2.10/2.8.0/casbah-core_2.10-2.8.0.jar ...
    [SUCCESSFUL ] org.mongodb#casbah-core_2.10;2.8.0!casbah-core_2.10.
jar (2785ms)
downloading https://repo1.maven.org/maven2/com/github/nscala-time/
nscala-time_2.10/1.0.0/nscala-time_2.10-1.0.0.jar ...
    [SUCCESSFUL ] com.github.nscala-time#nscala-time_2.10;1.0.0!nscala-
time_2.10.jar (2725ms)
downloading https://repo1.maven.org/maven2/org/slf4j/slf4j-api/1.6.0/
slf4j-api-1.6.0.jar ...
    [SUCCESSFUL ] org.slf4j#slf4j-api;1.6.0!slf4j-api.jar (371ms)
downloading https://repo1.maven.org/maven2/org/mongodb/mongo-java-
driver/2.13.0/mongo-java-driver-2.13.0.jar ...
    [SUCCESSFUL ] org.mongodb#mongo-java-driver;2.13.0!mongo-java-
driver.jar (5259ms)
downloading https://repo1.maven.org/maven2/joda-time/joda-time/2.3/
joda-time-2.3.jar ...
    [SUCCESSFUL ] joda-time#joda-time;2.3!joda-time.jar (6949ms)
downloading https://repo1.maven.org/maven2/org/joda/joda-convert/1.2/
joda-convert-1.2.jar ...
    [SUCCESSFUL ] org.joda#joda-convert;1.2!joda-convert.jar (548ms)
:: resolution report :: resolve 11850ms :: artifacts dl 26075ms
    :: modules in use:
  com.github.nscala-time#nscala-time_2.10;1.0.0 from central in
[default]
  com.stratio.datasource#spark-mongodb_2.10;0.10.1 from central in
[default]
  joda-time#joda-time;2.3 from central in [default]
  org.joda#joda-convert;1.2 from central in [default]
  org.mongodb#casbah-commons_2.10;2.8.0 from central in [default]
  org.mongodb#casbah-core_2.10;2.8.0 from central in [default]
  org.mongodb#casbah-query_2.10;2.8.0 from central in [default]
  org.mongodb#mongo-java-driver;2.13.0 from central in [default]
  org.slf4j#slf4j-api;1.6.0 from central in [default]
  ---------------------------------------------------------------
  --
```

```
|                      |        modules       ||  artifacts
|
|        conf     | number|  search|dwnlded|evicted||
number|dwnlded|
   --------------------------------------------------------------
--
|        default   |   9   |   9   |   9   |   0   ||   9   |   9
|
   --------------------------------------------------------------
--
:: retrieving :: org.apache.spark#spark-submit-parent
  confs: [default]
  9 artifacts copied, 0 already retrieved (2335kB/51ms)
... (snip) ...
```

We are now ready to query MongoDB on localhost:27017 from the collection twtr01_coll in the database twtr01_db.

We first import the SQLContext:

```
In [5]:
from pyspark.sql import SQLContext
sqlContext.sql("CREATE TEMPORARY TABLE tweet_table USING com.stratio.
datasource.mongodb OPTIONS (host 'localhost:27017', database 'twtr01_
db', collection 'twtr01_coll')")
sqlContext.sql("SELECT * FROM tweet_table where id=598830778269769728
").collect()
```

Here's the output of our query:

```
Out[5]:
[Row(text=u'@spark_io is now @particle - awesome news - now I can
enjoy my Particle Cores/Photons + @sparkfun sensors + @ApacheSpark
analytics :-)', _id=u'55aa640fd770871cba74cb88', contributors=None,
retweeted=False, user=Row(contributors_enabled=False, created_at=u'Mon
Aug 25 14:01:26 +0000 2008', default_profile=True, default_profile_
image=False, description=u'Building open source tools for and teaching
enterprise software developers', entities=Row(description=Row(ur
ls=[]), url=Row(urls=[Row(url=u'http://t.co/TSHp13EWeu', indices=[0,
22],

... (snip) ...
```

```
   9], name=u'Spark is Particle', screen_name=u'spark_io'),
Row(id=487010011, id_str=u'487010011', indices=[17, 26],
name=u'Particle', screen_name=u'particle'), Row(id=17877351,
id_str=u'17877351', indices=[88, 97], name=u'SparkFun
Electronics', screen_name=u'sparkfun'), Row(id=1551361069, id_
str=u'1551361069', indices=[108, 120], name=u'Apache Spark', screen_
name=u'ApacheSpark')]), is_quote_status=None, lang=u'en', quoted_
status_id_str=None, quoted_status_id=None, created_at=u'Thu May
14 12:42:37 +0000 2015', retweeted_status=None, truncated=False,
place=None, id=598830778269769728, in_reply_to_user_id=3187046084,
retweet_count=0, in_reply_to_status_id=None, in_reply_to_screen_
name=u'spark_io', in_reply_to_user_id_str=u'3187046084', source=u'<a
href="http://twitter.com" rel="nofollow">Twitter Web Client</a>',
id_str=u'598830778269769728', coordinates=None, metadata=Row(iso_
language_code=u'en', result_type=u'recent'), quoted_status=None)]
#
```

Summary

In this chapter, we harvested data from Twitter. Once the data was acquired, we explored the information using `Continuum.io`'s Blaze and Odo libraries. Spark SQL is an important module for interactive data exploration, analysis, and transformation, leveraging the Spark dataframe datastructure. The dataframe concept originates from R and then was adopted by Python Pandas with great success. The dataframe is the workhorse of the data scientist. The combination of Spark SQL and dataframe creates a powerful engine for data processing.

We are now gearing up for extracting the insights from the datasets using machine learning from Spark MLlib.

4
Learning from Data
Using Spark

As we have laid the foundation for data to be harvested in the previous chapter, we are now ready to learn from the data. Machine learning is about drawing insights from data. Our objective is to give an overview of the Spark **MLlib** (short for **Machine Learning library**) and apply the appropriate algorithms to our dataset in order to derive insights. From the Twitter dataset, we will be applying an unsupervised clustering algorithm in order to distinguish between Apache Spark-relevant tweets versus the rest. We have as initial input a mixed bag of tweets. We first need to preprocess the data in order to extract the relevant features, then apply the machine learning algorithm to our dataset, and finally evaluate the results and the performance of our model.

In this chapter, we will cover the following points:

- Providing an overview of the Spark MLlib module with its algorithms and the typical machine learning workflow.

- Preprocessing the Twitter harvested dataset to extract the relevant features, applying an unsupervised clustering algorithm to identify *Apache Spark-*relevant tweets. Then, evaluating the model and the results obtained.

- Describing the Spark machine learning pipeline.

Contextualizing Spark MLlib in the app architecture

Let's first contextualize the focus of this chapter on data-intensive app architecture. We will concentrate our attention on the analytics layer and more precisely machine learning. This will serve as a foundation for streaming apps as we want to apply the learning from the batch processing of data as inference rules for the streaming analysis.

The following diagram sets the context of the chapter's focus, highlighting the machine learning module within the analytics layer while using tools for exploratory data analysis, Spark SQL, and Pandas.

Data Intensive App Framework			
Engagement Layer			
Bokeh			Visualization (Charts, Time Series, Maps...)
Analytics Layer			
Spark SQL - Blaze *Exploration*	Spark MLlib *Machine Learning*	Spark GraphX *Graph*	Spark Streaming *Streaming*
Integration Layer			
Blaze – SparkSQL - Pandas			Connect – Collect – Correct – Compose – Consume
Persistence Layer			
MySQL - PostgreSQL *RDBMS*	Redis -HDFS *K-V Store - File Systems*	MongoDB *Document DB*	Cassandra *Columnar DB*
Infrastructure Layer			
VirtualBox - Vagrant *Virtualization*	Amazon Web Services Anaconda Cluster *Scalability*	Docker/Chef/Puppet/Ansible *Continuous Integration*	

Classifying Spark MLlib algorithms

Spark MLlib is a rapidly evolving module of Spark with new algorithms added with each release of Spark.

The following diagram provides a high-level overview of Spark MLlib algorithms grouped in the traditional broad machine learning techniques and following the categorical or continuous nature of the data:

Spark MLlib		
	Categorical Qualitative	**Continuous** Quantitative
Unsupervised Extracting structure	**Clustering** K-means	**Dimension Reduction** Singular Value Decomposition (SVD) Principal Component Analysis (PCA)
Supervised Making prediction	**Classification** Naive Bayes Decision Trees Ensembles of Trees (Random Forests and Gradient-Boosted Trees)	**Regression** linear models Support Vector Machines logistic regression linear regression
Recommender Associating user item	**Collaborative Filtering** Alternating Least Squares (ALS)	
Optimization Finding minima		**Optimization** Stochastic Gradient Descent Limited-memory BFGS (L-BFGS)
Feature Extraction Processing text	**Feature Extraction** **Transformation** TF-IDF - Word2Vec Standard Scaler - Normalizer	

We categorize the Spark MLlib algorithms in two columns, categorical or continuous, depending on the type of data. We distinguish between data that is categorical or more qualitative in nature versus continuous data, which is quantitative in nature. An example of qualitative data is predicting the weather; given the atmospheric pressure, the temperature, and the presence and type of clouds, the weather will be sunny, dry, rainy, or overcast. These are discrete values. On the other hand, let's say we want to predict house prices, given the location, square meterage, and the number of beds; the real estate value can be predicted using linear regression. In this case, we are talking about continuous or quantitative values.

The horizontal grouping reflects the types of machine learning method used. Unsupervised versus supervised machine learning techniques are dependent on whether the training data is labeled. In an unsupervised learning challenge, no labels are given to the learning algorithm. The goal is to find the hidden structure in its input. In the case of supervised learning, the data is labeled. The focus is on making predictions using regression if the data is continuous or classification if the data is categorical.

An important category of machine learning is recommender systems, which leverage collaborative filtering techniques. The Amazon web store and Netflix have very powerful recommender systems powering their recommendations.

Stochastic Gradient Descent is one of the machine learning optimization techniques that is well suited for Spark distributed computation.

For processing large amounts of text, Spark offers crucial libraries for feature extraction and transformation such as **TF-IDF** (short for **Term Frequency – Inverse Document Frequency**), Word2Vec, standard scaler, and normalizer.

Supervised and unsupervised learning

We delve more deeply here in to the traditional machine learning algorithms offered by Spark MLlib. We distinguish between supervised and unsupervised learning depending on whether the data is labeled. We distinguish between categorical or continuous depending on whether the data is discrete or continuous.

The following diagram explains the Spark MLlib supervised and unsupervised machine learning algorithms and preprocessing techniques:

Spark MLlib		
	Categorical Qualitative	**Continuous** Quantitative
Unsupervised Extracting structure	**Clustering** K-means	**Dimension Reduction** Singular Value Decomposition (SVD) Principal Component Analysis (PCA)
Supervised Making prediction	**Classification** Naive Bayes Decision Trees Ensembles of Trees (Random Forests and Gradient-Boosted Trees)	**Regression** linear models Support Vector Machines logistic regression linear regression

The following supervised and unsupervised MLlib algorithms and preprocessing techniques are currently available in Spark:

- **Clustering**: This is an unsupervised machine learning technique where the data is not labeled. The aim is to extract structure from the data:
    - ○ **K-Means**: This partitions the data in K distinct clusters
    - ○ **Gaussian Mixture**: Clusters are assigned based on the maximum posterior probability of the component
    - ○ **Power Iteration Clustering (PIC)**: This groups vertices of a graph based on pairwise edge similarities
    - ○ **Latent Dirichlet Allocation (LDA)**: This is used to group collections of text documents into topics
    - ○ **Streaming K-Means**: This means clusters dynamically streaming data using a windowing function on the incoming data

- **Dimensionality Reduction**: This aims to reduce the number of features under consideration. Essentially, this reduces noise in the data and focuses on the key features:
    - ○ **Singular Value Decomposition (SVD)**: This breaks the matrix that contains the data into simpler meaningful pieces. It factorizes the initial matrix into three matrices.
    - ○ **Principal Component Analysis (PCA)**: This approximates a high dimensional dataset with a low dimensional sub space.

- **Regression and Classification**: Regression predicts output values using labeled training data, while Classification groups the results into classes. Classification has dependent variables that are categorical or unordered whilst Regression has dependent variables that are continuous and ordered:

  ° **Linear Regression Models** (linear regression, logistic regression, and support vector machines): Linear regression algorithms can be expressed as convex optimization problems that aim to minimize an objective function based on a vector of weight variables. The objective function controls the complexity of the model through the regularized part of the function and the error of the model through the loss part of the function.

  ° **Naive Bayes**: This makes predictions based on the conditional probability distribution of a label given an observation. It assumes that features are mutually independent of each other.

  ° **Decision Trees**: This performs recursive binary partitioning of the feature space. The information gain at the tree node level is maximized in order to determine the best split for the partition.

  ° **Ensembles of trees** (Random Forests and Gradient-Boosted Trees): Tree ensemble algorithms combine base decision tree models in order to build a performant model. They are intuitive and very successful for classification and regression tasks.

- **Isotonic Regression**: This minimizes the mean squared error between given data and observed responses.

Additional learning algorithms

Spark MLlib offers more algorithms than the supervised and unsupervised learning ones. We have broadly three more additional types of machine learning methods: recommender systems, optimization algorithms, and feature extraction.

Spark MLlib		
	Categorical Qualitative	**Continuous** Quantitative
Recommender Associating user item	Collaborative Filtering Alternating Least Squares (ALS)	
Optimization Finding minima		Optimization Stochastic Gradient Descent Limited-memory BFGS (L-BFGS)
Feature Extraction Processing text	Feature Extraction Transformation TF-IDF - Word2Vec Standard Scaler - Normalizer	

The following additional MLlib algorithms are currently available in Spark:

- **Collaborative filtering**: This is the basis for recommender systems. It creates a user-item association matrix and aims to fill the gaps. Based on other users and items along with their ratings, it recommends an item that the target user has no ratings for. In distributed computing, one of the most successful algorithms is **ALS** (short for **Alternating Least Square**):

  - **Alternating Least Squares**: This matrix factorization technique incorporates implicit feedback, temporal effects, and confidence levels. It decomposes the large user item matrix into a lower dimensional user and item factors. It minimizes a quadratic loss function by fixing alternatively its factors.

- **Feature extraction and transformation**: These are essential techniques for large text document processing. It includes the following techniques:

  - **Term Frequency**: Search engines use TF-IDF to score and rank document relevance in a vast corpus. It is also used in machine learning to determine the importance of a word in a document or corpus. Term frequency statistically determines the weight of a term relative to its frequency in the corpus. Term frequency on its own can be misleading as it overemphasizes words such as *the*, *of*, or *and* that give little information. Inverse Document Frequency provides the specificity or the measure of the amount of information, whether the term is rare or common across all documents in the corpus.

- ° **Word2Vec**: This includes two models, **Skip-Gram** and **Continuous Bag of Word**. The Skip-Gram predicts neighboring words given a word, based on sliding windows of words, while Continuous Bag of Words predicts the current word given the neighboring words.

- ° **Standard Scaler**: As part of preprocessing, the dataset must often be standardized by mean removal and variance scaling. We compute the mean and standard deviation on the training data and apply the same transformation to the test data.

- ° **Normalizer**: We scale the samples to have unit norm. It is useful for quadratic forms such as the dot product or kernel methods.

- ° **Feature selection**: This reduces the dimensionality of the vector space by selecting the most relevant features for the model.

- ° **Chi-Square Selector**: This is a statistical method to measure the independence of two events.

- **Optimization**: These specific Spark MLlib optimization algorithms focus on various techniques of gradient descent. Spark provides very efficient implementation of gradient descent on a distributed cluster of machines. It looks for the local minima by iteratively going down the steepest descent. It is compute-intensive as it iterates through all the data available:

  - ° **Stochastic Gradient Descent**: We minimize an objective function that is the sum of differentiable functions. Stochastic Gradient Descent uses only a sample of the training data in order to update a parameter in a particular iteration. It is used for large-scale and sparse machine learning problems such as text classification.

- **Limited-memory BFGS (L-BFGS)**: As the name says, L-BFGS uses limited memory and suits the distributed optimization algorithm implementation of Spark MLlib.

Spark MLlib data types

MLlib supports four essential data types: **local vector**, **labeled point**, **local matrix**, and **distributed matrix**. These data types are widely used in Spark MLlib algorithms:

- **Local vector**: This resides in a single machine. It can be dense or sparse:

  - ° Dense vector is a traditional array of doubles. An example of dense vector is [5.0, 0.0, 1.0, 7.0].

  - ° Sparse vector uses integer indices and double values. So the sparse representation of the vector [5.0, 0.0, 1.0, 7.0] would be (4, [0, 2, 3], [5.0, 1.0, 7.0]), where represent the dimension of the vector.

Here's an example of local vector in PySpark:

```
import numpy as np
import scipy.sparse as sps
from pyspark.mllib.linalg import Vectors

# NumPy array for dense vector.
dvect1 = np.array([5.0, 0.0, 1.0, 7.0])
# Python list for dense vector.
dvect2 = [5.0, 0.0, 1.0, 7.0]
# SparseVector creation
svect1 = Vectors.sparse(4, [0, 2, 3], [5.0, 1.0, 7.0])
# Sparse vector using a single-column SciPy csc_matrix
svect2 = sps.csc_matrix((np.array([5.0, 1.0, 7.0]), np.array([0,
2, 3])), shape = (4, 1))
```

- **Labeled point**. A labeled point is a dense or sparse vector with a label used in supervised learning. In the case of binary labels, 0.0 represents the negative label whilst 1.0 represents the positive value.

  Here's an example of a labeled point in PySpark:

```
from pyspark.mllib.linalg import SparseVector
from pyspark.mllib.regression import LabeledPoint

# Labeled point with a positive label and a dense feature vector.
lp_pos = LabeledPoint(1.0, [5.0, 0.0, 1.0, 7.0])

# Labeled point with a negative label and a sparse feature vector.
lp_neg = LabeledPoint(0.0, SparseVector(4, [0, 2, 3], [5.0, 1.0,
7.0]))
```

- **Local Matrix**: This local matrix resides in a single machine with integer-type indices and values of type double.

  Here's an example of a local matrix in PySpark:

```
from pyspark.mllib.linalg import Matrix, Matrices

# Dense matrix ((1.0, 2.0, 3.0), (4.0, 5.0, 6.0))
dMatrix = Matrices.dense(2, 3, [1, 2, 3, 4, 5, 6])

# Sparse matrix ((9.0, 0.0), (0.0, 8.0), (0.0, 6.0))
sMatrix = Matrices.sparse(3, 2, [0, 1, 3], [0, 2, 1], [9, 6, 8])
```

- **Distributed Matrix**: Leveraging the distributed mature of the RDD, distributed matrices can be shared in a cluster of machines. We distinguish four distributed matrix types: `RowMatrix`, `IndexedRowMatrix`, `CoordinateMatrix`, and `BlockMatrix`:

    ° `RowMatrix`: This takes an RDD of vectors and creates a distributed matrix of rows with meaningless indices, called `RowMatrix`, from the RDD of vectors.

    ° `IndexedRowMatrix`: In this case, row indices are meaningful. First, we create an RDD of indexed rows using the class `IndexedRow` and then create an `IndexedRowMatrix`.

    ° `CoordinateMatrix`: This is useful to represent very large and very sparse matrices. `CoordinateMatrix` is created from RDDs of the `MatrixEntry` points, represented by a tuple of type (long, long, or float)

    ° `BlockMatrix`: These are created from RDDs of sub-matrix blocks, where a sub-matrix block is `((blockRowIndex, blockColIndex), sub-matrix)`.

Machine learning workflows and data flows

Beyond algorithms, machine learning is also about processes. We will discuss the typical workflows and data flows of supervised and unsupervised machine learning.

Supervised machine learning workflows

In supervised machine learning, the input training dataset is labeled. One of the key data practices is to split input data into training and test sets, and validate the mode accordingly.

We typically go through a six-step process flow in supervised learning:

- **Collect the data**: This step essentially ties in with the previous chapter and ensures we collect the right data with the right volume and granularity in order to enable the machine learning algorithm to provide reliable answers.

- **Preprocess the data**: This step is about checking the data quality by sampling, filling in the missing values if any, scaling and normalizing the data. We also define the feature extraction process. Typically, in the case of large text-based datasets, we apply tokenization, stop words removal, stemming, and TF-IDF.

  In the case of supervised learning, we separate the input data into a training and test set. We can also implement various strategies of sampling and splitting the dataset for cross-validation purposes.

- **Ready the data**: In this step, we get the data in the format or data type expected by the algorithms. In the case of Spark MLlib, this includes local vector, dense or sparse vectors, labeled points, local matrix, distributed matrix with row matrix, indexed row matrix, coordinate matrix, and block matrix.

- **Model**: In this step, we apply the algorithms that are suitable for the problem at hand and get the results for evaluation of the most suitable algorithm in the evaluate step. We might have multiple algorithms suitable for the problem; their respective performance will be scored in the evaluate step to select the best preforming ones. We can implement an ensemble or combination of models in order to reach the best results.

- **Optimize**: We may need to run a grid search for the optimal parameters of certain algorithms. These parameters are determined during training, and fine-tuned during the testing and production phase.

- **Evaluate**: We ultimately score the models and select the best one in terms of accuracy, performance, reliability, and scalability. We move the best performing model to test with the held out test data in order to ascertain the prediction accuracy of our model. Once satisfied with the fine-tuned model, we move it to production to process live data.

The supervised machine learning workflow and dataflow are represented in the following diagram:

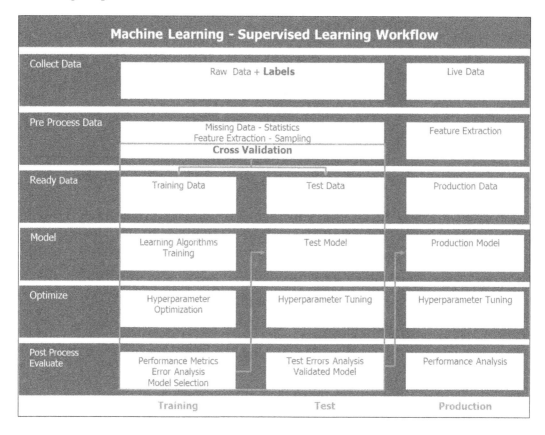

Unsupervised machine learning workflows

As opposed to supervised learning, our initial data is not labeled in the case of unsupervised learning, which is most often the case in real life. We will extract the structure from the data by using clustering or dimensionality reduction algorithms. In the unsupervised learning case, we do not split the data into training and test, as we cannot make any prediction because the data is not labeled. We will train the data along six steps similar to those in supervised learning. Once the model is trained, we will evaluate the results and fine-tune the model and then release it for production.

Unsupervised learning can be a preliminary step to supervised learning. Namely, we look at reducing the dimensionality of the data prior to attacking the learning phase.

The unsupervised machine learning workflows and dataflow are represented as follows:

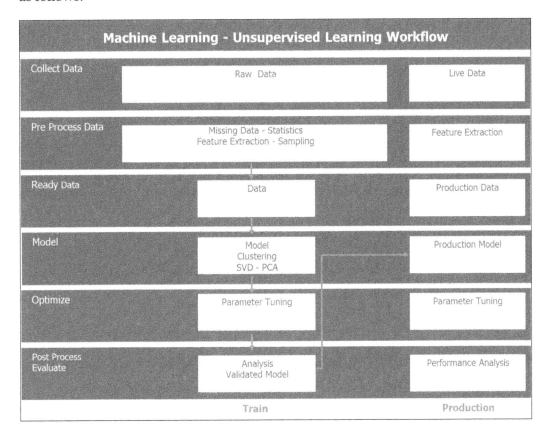

Clustering the Twitter dataset

Let's first get a feel for the data extracted from Twitter and get an understanding of the data structure in order to prepare and run it through the K-Means clustering algorithms. Our plan of attack uses the process and dataflow depicted earlier for unsupervised learning. The steps are as follows:

1. Combine all tweet files into a single dataframe.

2. Parse the tweets, remove stop words, extract emoticons, extract URL, and finally normalize the words (for example, mapping them to lowercase and removing punctuation and numbers).

3. Feature extraction includes the following:

   ° **Tokenization**: This breaks down the parsed tweet text into individual words or tokens

   ° **TF-IDF**: This applies the TF-IDF algorithm to create feature vectors from the tokenized tweet texts

   ° **Hash TF-IDF**: This applies a hashing function to the token vectors

4. Run the K-Means clustering algorithm.

5. Evaluate the results of the K-Means clustering:

   ° Identify tweet membership to clusters

   ° Perform dimensionality reduction to two dimensions with the Multi-Dimensional Scaling or the Principal Component Analysis algorithm

   ° Plot the clusters

6. Pipeline:

   ° Fine-tune the number of relevant clusters K

   ° Measure the model cost

   ° Select the optimal model

Applying Scikit-Learn on the Twitter dataset

Python's own Scikit-Learn machine learning library is one of the most reliable, intuitive, and robust tools around. Let's run through a preprocessing and unsupervised learning using Pandas and Scikit-Learn. It is often beneficial to explore a sample of the data using Scikit-Learn before spinning off clusters with Spark MLlib.

We have a mixed bag of 7,540 tweets. It contains tweets related to Apache Spark, Python, the upcoming presidential election with Hillary Clinton and Donald Trump as protagonists, and some tweets related to fashion and music with Lady Gaga and Justin Bieber. We are running the K-Means clustering algorithm using Python Scikit-Learn on the Twitter dataset harvested. We first load the sample data into a Pandas dataframe:

```
import pandas as pd

csv_in = 'C:\\Users\\Amit\\Documents\\IPython Notebooks\\AN00_Data\\
unq_tweetstxt.csv'
twts_df01 = pd.read_csv(csv_in, sep =';', encoding='utf-8')

In [24]:
```

```
twts_df01.count()
Out[24]:
Unnamed: 0     7540
id             7540
created_at     7540
user_id        7540
user_name      7538
tweet_text     7540
dtype: int64


#
# Introspecting the tweets text
#
In [82]:


twtstxt_ls01[6910:6920]
Out[82]:
['RT @deroach_Ismoke: I am NOT voting for #hilaryclinton http://t.co/
jaZZpcHkkJ',
 'RT @AnimalRightsJen: #HilaryClinton What do Bernie Sanders and
Donald Trump Have in Common?: He has so far been th... http://t.co/
t2YRcGCh6…',
 'I understand why Bill was out banging other chicks........I mean
look at what he is married to.....\n@HilaryClinton',
 '#HilaryClinton What do Bernie Sanders and Donald Trump Have in
Common?: He has so far been th... http://t.co/t2YRcGCh67 #Tcot
#UniteBlue']
```

We first perform a feature extraction from the tweets' text. We apply a sparse vectorizer to the dataset using a TF-IDF vectorizer with 10,000 features and English stop words:

```
In [37]:


print("Extracting features from the training dataset using a sparse
vectorizer")
t0 = time()
Extracting features from the training dataset using a sparse
vectorizer
In [38]:


vectorizer = TfidfVectorizer(max_df=0.5, max_features=10000,
                             min_df=2, stop_words='english',
                             use_idf=True)
X = vectorizer.fit_transform(twtstxt_ls01)
#
```

```
# Output of the TFIDF Feature vectorizer
#
print("done in %fs" % (time() - t0))
print("n_samples: %d, n_features: %d" % X.shape)
print()
done in 5.232165s
n_samples: 7540, n_features: 6638
```

As the dataset is now broken into a 7540 sample with vectors of 6,638 features, we are ready to feed this sparse matrix to the K-Means clustering algorithm. We will choose seven clusters and 100 maximum iterations initially:

```
In [47]:

km = KMeans(n_clusters=7, init='k-means++', max_iter=100, n_init=1,
            verbose=1)

print("Clustering sparse data with %s" % km)
t0 = time()
km.fit(X)
print("done in %0.3fs" % (time() - t0))

Clustering sparse data with KMeans(copy_x=True, init='k-means++', max_
iter=100, n_clusters=7, n_init=1,
    n_jobs=1, precompute_distances='auto', random_state=None,
tol=0.0001,
    verbose=1)
Initialization complete
Iteration  0, inertia 13635.141
Iteration  1, inertia 6943.485
Iteration  2, inertia 6924.093
Iteration  3, inertia 6915.004
Iteration  4, inertia 6909.212
Iteration  5, inertia 6903.848
Iteration  6, inertia 6888.606
Iteration  7, inertia 6863.226
Iteration  8, inertia 6860.026
Iteration  9, inertia 6859.338
Iteration 10, inertia 6859.213
Iteration 11, inertia 6859.102
Iteration 12, inertia 6859.080
Iteration 13, inertia 6859.060
Iteration 14, inertia 6859.047
Iteration 15, inertia 6859.039
Iteration 16, inertia 6859.032
```

```
Iteration 17, inertia 6859.031
Iteration 18, inertia 6859.029
Converged at iteration 18
done in 1.701s
```

The K-Means clustering algorithm converged after 18 iterations. We see in the following results the seven clusters with their respective key words. Clusters 0 and 6 are about music and fashion with Justin Bieber and Lady Gaga-related tweets. Clusters 1 and 5 are related to the U.S.A. presidential elections with Donald Trump- and Hilary Clinton-related tweets. Clusters 2 and 3 are the ones of interest to us as they are about Apache Spark and Python. Cluster 4 contains Thailand-related tweets:

```
#
# Introspect top terms per cluster
#

In [49]:

print("Top terms per cluster:")
order_centroids = km.cluster_centers_.argsort()[:, ::-1]
terms = vectorizer.get_feature_names()
for i in range(7):
    print("Cluster %d:" % i, end='')
    for ind in order_centroids[i, :20]:
        print(' %s' % terms[ind], end='')
    print()
Top terms per cluster:
Cluster 0: justinbieber love mean rt follow thank hi https
whatdoyoumean video wanna hear whatdoyoumeanviral rorykramer happy lol
making person dream justin
Cluster 1: donaldtrump hilaryclinton rt https trump2016
realdonaldtrump trump gop amp justinbieber president clinton emails
oy8ltkstze tcot like berniesanders hilary people email
Cluster 2: bigdata apachespark hadoop analytics rt spark training
chennai ibm datascience apache processing cloudera mapreduce data sap
https vora transforming development
Cluster 3: apachespark python https rt spark data amp databricks using
new learn hadoop ibm big apache continuumio bluemix learning join open
Cluster 4: ernestsgantt simbata3 jdhm2015 elsahel12 phuketdailynews
dreamintentions beyhiveinfrance almtorta18 civipartnership 9_a_6
25whu72ep0 k7erhvu7wn fdmxxxcm3h osxuh2fxnt 5o5rmb0xhp jnbgkqn0dj
ovap57ujdh dtzsz3lb6x sunnysai12345 sdcvulih6g
Cluster 5: trump donald donaldtrump starbucks trumpquote
trumpforpresident oy8ltkstze https zfns7pxysx silly goy stump
trump2016 news jeremy coffee corbyn ok7vc8aetz rt tonight
Cluster 6: ladygaga gaga lady rt https love follow horror cd story
ahshotel american japan hotel human trafficking music fashion diet
queen ahs
```

We will visualize the results by plotting the cluster. We have 7,540 samples with 6,638 features. It will be impossible to visualize that many dimensions. We will use the **Multi-Dimensional Scaling (MDS)** algorithm to bring down the multidimensional features of the clusters into two tractable dimensions to be able to picture them:

```python
import matplotlib.pyplot as plt
import matplotlib as mpl
from sklearn.manifold import MDS

MDS()

#
# Bring down the MDS to two dimensions (components) as we will plot
# the clusters
#
mds = MDS(n_components=2, dissimilarity="precomputed", random_state=1)

pos = mds.fit_transform(dist)  # shape (n_components, n_samples)

xs, ys = pos[:, 0], pos[:, 1]

In [67]:

#
# Set up colors per clusters using a dict
#
cluster_colors = {0: '#1b9e77', 1: '#d95f02', 2: '#7570b3', 3:
'#e7298a', 4: '#66a61e', 5: '#9990b3', 6: '#e8888a'}

#
#set up cluster names using a dict
#
cluster_names = {0: 'Music, Pop',
                 1: 'USA Politics, Election',
                 2: 'BigData, Spark',
                 3: 'Spark, Python',
                 4: 'Thailand',
                 5: 'USA Politics, Election',
                 6: 'Music, Pop'}
In [115]:
#
# ipython magic to show the matplotlib plots inline
#
```

```
%matplotlib inline

#
# Create data frame which includes MDS results, cluster numbers and
tweet texts to be displayed
#
df = pd.DataFrame(dict(x=xs, y=ys, label=clusters, txt=twtstxt_ls02_
utf8))
ix_start = 2000
ix_stop  = 2050
df01 = df[ix_start:ix_stop]

print(df01[['label','txt']])
print(len(df01))
print()

# Group by cluster

groups = df.groupby('label')
groups01 = df01.groupby('label')

# Set up the plot

fig, ax = plt.subplots(figsize=(17, 10))
ax.margins(0.05)

#
# Build the plot object
#
for name, group in groups01:
    ax.plot(group.x, group.y, marker='o', linestyle='', ms=12,
            label=cluster_names[name], color=cluster_colors[name],
            mec='none')
    ax.set_aspect('auto')
    ax.tick_params(\
        axis= 'x',          # settings for x-axis
        which='both',       #
        bottom='off',       #
        top='off',          #
        labelbottom='off')
    ax.tick_params(\
        axis= 'y',          # settings for y-axis
        which='both',       #
```

```
        left='off',        #
        top='off',         #
        labelleft='off')

ax.legend(numpoints=1)     #
#
# Add label in x,y position with tweet text
#
for i in range(ix_start, ix_stop):
    ax.text(df01.ix[i]['x'], df01.ix[i]['y'], df01.ix[i]['txt'],
size=10)

plt.show()                 # Display the plot
```

```
      label       text
2000    2         b'RT @BigDataTechCon: '
2001    3         b"@4Quant 's presentat"
2002    2         b'Cassandra Summit 201'
```

Here's a plot of Cluster 2, *Big Data* and *Spark.*, represented by blue dots along with Cluster 3, *Spark* and *Python*, represented by red dots, and some sample tweets related to the respective clusters:

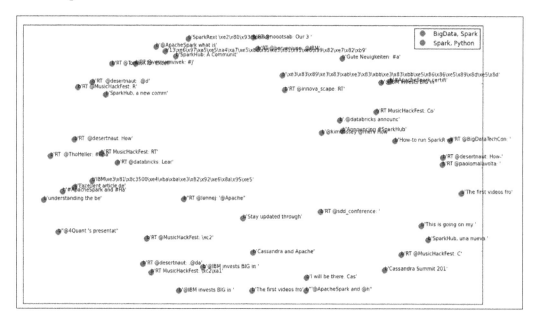

We have gained some good insights into the data with the exploration and processing done with Scikit-Learn. We will now focus our attention on Spark MLlib and take it for a ride on the Twitter dataset.

Preprocessing the dataset

Now, we will focus on feature extraction and engineering in order to ready the data for the clustering algorithm run. We instantiate the Spark Context and read the Twitter dataset into a Spark dataframe. We will then successively tokenize the tweet text data, apply a hashing Term frequency algorithm to the tokens, and finally apply the Inverse Document Frequency algorithm and rescale the data. The code is as follows:

```
In [3]:
#
# Read csv in a Panda DF
#
#
import pandas as pd
csv_in = '/home/an/spark/spark-1.5.0-bin-hadoop2.6/examples/AN_Spark/
data/unq_tweetstxt.csv'
pddf_in = pd.read_csv(csv_in, index_col=None, header=0, sep=';',
encoding='utf-8')

In [4]:

sqlContext = SQLContext(sc)

In [5]:

#
# Convert a Panda DF to a Spark DF
#
#

spdf_02 = sqlContext.createDataFrame(pddf_in[['id', 'user_id', 'user_
name', 'tweet_text']])

In [8]:

spdf_02.show()

In [7]:
```

```
spdf_02.take(3)
```

```
Out[7]:
```

```
[Row(id=638830426971181057, user_id=3276255125, user_name=u'True
Equality', tweet_text=u'ernestsgantt: BeyHiveInFrance: 9_A_6:
dreamintentions: elsahel12: simbata3: JDHM2015: almtorta18:
dreamintentions:\u2026 http://t.co/VpD7FoqMr0'),
 Row(id=638830426727911424, user_id=3276255125, user_name=u'True
Equality', tweet_text=u'ernestsgantt: BeyHiveInFrance:
PhuketDailyNews: dreamintentions: elsahel12: simbata3: JDHM2015:
almtorta18: CiviPa\u2026 http://t.co/VpD7FoqMr0'),
 Row(id=638830425402556417, user_id=3276255125, user_name=u'True
Equality', tweet_text=u'ernestsgantt: BeyHiveInFrance: 9_A_6:
ernestsgantt: elsahel12: simbata3: JDHM2015: almtorta18:
CiviPartnership: dr\u2026 http://t.co/EMDOn8chPK')]
```

```
In [9]:
```

```
from pyspark.ml.feature import HashingTF, IDF, Tokenizer
```

```
In [10]:
```

```
#
# Tokenize the tweet_text
#
tokenizer = Tokenizer(inputCol="tweet_text", outputCol="tokens")
tokensData = tokenizer.transform(spdf_02)
```

```
In [11]:
```

```
tokensData.take(1)
```

```
Out[11]:
```

```
[Row(id=638830426971181057, user_id=3276255125, user_name=u'True
Equality', tweet_text=u'ernestsgantt: BeyHiveInFrance:
9_A_6: dreamintentions: elsahel12: simbata3: JDHM2015:
almtorta18: dreamintentions:\u2026 http://t.co/VpD7FoqMr0',
tokens=[u'ernestsgantt:', u'beyhiveinfrance:', u'9_a_6:',
u'dreamintentions:', u'elsahel12:', u'simbata3:', u'jdhm2015:',
u'almtorta18:', u'dreamintentions:\u2026', u'http://t.co/
vpd7foqmr0'])]
```

```
In [14]:
```

```
#
# Apply Hashing TF to the tokens
#
hashingTF = HashingTF(inputCol="tokens", outputCol="rawFeatures",
numFeatures=2000)
featuresData = hashingTF.transform(tokensData)
```

In [15]:

```
featuresData.take(1)
```

Out[15]:

```
[Row(id=638830426971181057, user_id=3276255125, user_name=u'True
Equality', tweet_text=u'ernestsgantt: BeyHiveInFrance:
9_A_6: dreamintentions: elsahel12: simbata3: JDHM2015:
almtorta18: dreamintentions:\u2026 http://t.co/VpD7FoqMr0',
tokens=[u'ernestsgantt:', u'beyhiveinfrance:', u'9_a_6:',
u'dreamintentions:', u'elsahel12:', u'simbata3:', u'jdhm2015:',
u'almtorta18:', u'dreamintentions:\u2026', u'http://t.co/vpd7foqmr0'],
rawFeatures=SparseVector(2000, {74: 1.0, 97: 1.0, 100: 1.0, 160: 1.0,
185: 1.0, 742: 1.0, 856: 1.0, 991: 1.0, 1383: 1.0, 1620: 1.0}))]
```

In [16]:

```
#
# Apply IDF to the raw features and rescale the data
#
idf = IDF(inputCol="rawFeatures", outputCol="features")
idfModel = idf.fit(featuresData)
rescaledData = idfModel.transform(featuresData)

for features in rescaledData.select("features").take(3):
  print(features)
```

In [17]:

```
rescaledData.take(2)
```

Out[17]:

```
[Row(id=638830426971181057, user_id=3276255125, user_name=u'True
Equality', tweet_text=u'ernestsgantt: BeyHiveInFrance:
9_A_6: dreamintentions: elsahel12: simbata3: JDHM2015:
almtorta18: dreamintentions:\u2026 http://t.co/VpD7FoqMr0',
tokens=[u'ernestsgantt:', u'beyhiveinfrance:', u'9_a_6:',
```

```
u'dreamintentions:', u'elsahel12:', u'simbata3:', u'jdhm2015:',
u'almtorta18:', u'dreamintentions:\u2026', u'http://t.co/vpd7foqmr0'],
rawFeatures=SparseVector(2000, {74: 1.0, 97: 1.0, 100: 1.0, 160:
1.0, 185: 1.0, 742: 1.0, 856: 1.0, 991: 1.0, 1383: 1.0, 1620: 1.0}),
features=SparseVector(2000, {74: 2.6762, 97: 1.8625, 100: 2.6384, 160:
2.9985, 185: 2.7481, 742: 5.5269, 856: 4.1406, 991: 2.9518, 1383:
4.694, 1620: 3.073})),
 Row(id=638830426727911424, user_id=3276255125, user_name=u'True
Equality', tweet_text=u'ernestsgantt: BeyHiveInFrance:
PhuketDailyNews: dreamintentions: elsahel12: simbata3:
JDHM2015: almtorta18: CiviPa\u2026 http://t.co/VpD7FoqMr0',
tokens=[u'ernestsgantt:', u'beyhiveinfrance:', u'phuketdailynews:',
u'dreamintentions:', u'elsahel12:', u'simbata3:', u'jdhm2015:',
u'almtorta18:', u'civipa\u2026', u'http://t.co/vpd7foqmr0'],
rawFeatures=SparseVector(2000, {74: 1.0, 97: 1.0, 100: 1.0, 160:
1.0, 185: 1.0, 460: 1.0, 987: 1.0, 991: 1.0, 1383: 1.0, 1620: 1.0}),
features=SparseVector(2000, {74: 2.6762, 97: 1.8625, 100: 2.6384,
160: 2.9985, 185: 2.7481, 460: 6.4432, 987: 2.9959, 991: 2.9518, 1383:
4.694, 1620: 3.073}))]
```

```
In [21]:

rs_pddf = rescaledData.toPandas()

In [22]:

rs_pddf.count()

Out[22]:

id           7540
user_id      7540
user_name    7540
tweet_text   7540
tokens       7540
rawFeatures  7540
features     7540
dtype: int64


In [27]:

feat_lst = rs_pddf.features.tolist()

In [28]:
```

```
feat_lst[:2]
```

```
Out[28]:
```

```
[SparseVector(2000, {74: 2.6762, 97: 1.8625, 100: 2.6384, 160: 2.9985,
185: 2.7481, 742: 5.5269, 856: 4.1406, 991: 2.9518, 1383: 4.694, 1620:
3.073}),
 SparseVector(2000, {74: 2.6762, 97: 1.8625, 100: 2.6384, 160: 2.9985,
185: 2.7481, 460: 6.4432, 987: 2.9959, 991: 2.9518, 1383: 4.694, 1620:
3.073})]
```

Running the clustering algorithm

We will use the K-Means algorithm against the Twitter dataset. As an unlabeled and shuffled bag of tweets, we want to see if the *Apache Spark* tweets are grouped in a single cluster. From the previous steps, the TF-IDF sparse vector of features is converted into an RDD that will be the input to the Spark MLlib program. We initialize the K-Means model with 5 clusters, 10 iterations of 10 runs:

```
In [32]:
```

```
from pyspark.mllib.clustering import KMeans, KMeansModel
from numpy import array
from math import sqrt
```

```
In [34]:
```

```
# Load and parse the data


in_Data = sc.parallelize(feat_lst)
```

```
In [35]:
```

```
in_Data.take(3)
```

```
Out[35]:
```

```
[SparseVector(2000, {74: 2.6762, 97: 1.8625, 100: 2.6384, 160: 2.9985,
185: 2.7481, 742: 5.5269, 856: 4.1406, 991: 2.9518, 1383: 4.694, 1620:
3.073}),
 SparseVector(2000, {74: 2.6762, 97: 1.8625, 100: 2.6384, 160: 2.9985,
185: 2.7481, 460: 6.4432, 987: 2.9959, 991: 2.9518, 1383: 4.694, 1620:
3.073}),
```

```
    SparseVector(2000, {20: 4.3534, 74: 2.6762, 97: 1.8625, 100: 5.2768,
    185: 2.7481, 856: 4.1406, 991: 2.9518, 1039: 3.073, 1620: 3.073, 1864:
    4.6377})]
```

```
In [37]:
```

```
in_Data.count()
```

```
Out[37]:
```

```
7540
```

```
In [38]:
```

```
# Build the model (cluster the data)
```

```
clusters = KMeans.train(in_Data, 5, maxIterations=10,
        runs=10, initializationMode="random")
```

```
In [53]:
```

```
# Evaluate clustering by computing Within Set Sum of Squared Errors
```

```
def error(point):
    center = clusters.centers[clusters.predict(point)]
    return sqrt(sum([x**2 for x in (point - center)]))
```

```
WSSSE = in_Data.map(lambda point: error(point)).reduce(lambda x, y: x
+ y)
print("Within Set Sum of Squared Error = " + str(WSSSE))
```

Evaluating the model and the results

One way to fine-tune the clustering algorithm is by varying the number of clusters and verifying the output. Let's check the clusters and get a feel for the clustering results so far:

```
In [43]:
```

```
cluster_membership = in_Data.map(lambda x: clusters.predict(x))
```

```
In [54]:
```

```
cluster_idx = cluster_membership.zipWithIndex()
```

In [55]:

```
type(cluster_idx)
```

Out[55]:

```
pyspark.rdd.PipelinedRDD
```

In [58]:

```
cluster_idx.take(20)
```

Out[58]:

```
[(3, 0),
 (3, 1),
 (3, 2),
 (3, 3),
 (3, 4),
 (3, 5),
 (1, 6),
 (3, 7),
 (3, 8),
 (3, 9),
 (3, 10),
 (3, 11),
 (3, 12),
 (3, 13),
 (3, 14),
 (1, 15),
 (3, 16),
 (3, 17),
 (1, 18),
 (1, 19)]
```

In [59]:

```
cluster_df = cluster_idx.toDF()
```

In [65]:

```
pddf_with_cluster = pd.concat([pddf_in, cluster_pddf],axis=1)
```

In [76]:

```
pddf_with_cluster._1.unique()
```

Out[76]:

```
array([3, 1, 4, 0, 2])
```

In [79]:

```
pddf_with_cluster[pddf_with_cluster['_1'] == 0].head(10)
```

Out[79]:
```
  Unnamed: 0   id    created_at    user_id    user_name    tweet_text    _1
_2
6227    3    642418116819988480    Fri Sep 11 19:23:09 +0000 2015
49693598    Ajinkya Kale    RT @bigdata: Distributed Matrix Computations
i...    0    6227
6257    45    642391207205859328    Fri Sep 11 17:36:13 +0000 2015
937467860    Angela Bassa    [Auto] I'm reading ""Distributed Matrix
Comput...    0    6257
6297    119    642348577147064320    Fri Sep 11 14:46:49 +0000
2015    18318677    Ben Lorica    Distributed Matrix Computations in @
ApacheSpar...    0    6297
```
In [80]:

```
pddf_with_cluster[pddf_with_cluster['_1'] == 1].head(10)
```

Out[80]:
```
  Unnamed: 0   id    created_at    user_id    user_name    tweet_text    _1
_2
6    6    638830419090079746    Tue Sep 01 21:46:55 +0000 2015
2241040634    Massimo Carrisi    Python:Python: Removing \xa0 from
string? - I ...    1    6
15    17    638830380578045953    Tue Sep 01 21:46:46 +0000 2015
57699376    Rafael Monnerat    RT @ramalhoorg: Noite de autógrafos do
Fluent ...    1    15
18    41    638830280988426250    Tue Sep 01 21:46:22 +0000 2015
951081582    Jack Baldwin    RT @cloudaus: We are 3/4 full! 2-day @
swcarpen...    1    18
19    42    638830276626399232    Tue Sep 01 21:46:21 +0000 2015
6525302    Masayoshi Nakamura    PynamoDB #AWS #DynamoDB #Python
http://...    1    19
```

```
20    43    638830213288235008    Tue Sep 01 21:46:06 +0000 2015
3153874869    Baltimore Python    Flexx: Python UI tookit based on web
technolog...    1    20
21    44    638830017645516800    Tue Sep 01 21:45:43 +0000 2015
48474625    Radio Free Denali    Hmm, emerge --depclean wants to remove
somethi...    1    21
22    46    638829977014636544    Tue Sep 01 21:45:10 +0000 2015
154915461    Luciano Ramalho    Noite de autógrafos do Fluent Python no
Garoa ...    1    22
23    47    638829882928070656    Tue Sep 01 21:44:47 +0000 2015
917320920    bsbafflesbrains    @DanSWright Harper channeling Monty
Python. "...    1    23
24    48    638829868679954432    Tue Sep 01 21:44:44 +0000 2015
134280898    Lannick Technology    RT @SergeyKalnish: I am #hiring:
Senior Back e...    1    24
25    49    638829707484508161    Tue Sep 01 21:44:05 +0000 2015
2839203454    Joshua Jones    RT @LindseyPelas: Surviving Monty Python
in Fl...    1    25
In [81]:
```

```
pddf_with_cluster[pddf_with_cluster['_1'] == 2].head(10)
```

```
Out[81]:
   Unnamed: 0    id    created_at    user_id    user_name    tweet_text    _1
_2
7280    688    639056941592014848    Wed Sep 02 12:47:02 +0000 2015
2735137484    Chris    A true gay icon when will @ladygaga @Madonna @...
2    7280
In [82]:
```

```
pddf_with_cluster[pddf_with_cluster['_1'] == 3].head(10)
```

```
Out[82]:
   Unnamed: 0    id    created_at    user_id    user_name    tweet_text    _1
_2
0    0    638830426971181057    Tue Sep 01 21:46:57 +0000 2015
3276255125    True Equality    ernestsgantt: BeyHiveInFrance: 9_A_6:
dreamint...    3    0
1    1    638830426727911424    Tue Sep 01 21:46:57 +0000 2015
3276255125    True Equality    ernestsgantt: BeyHiveInFrance:
PhuketDailyNews...    3    1
2    2    638830425402556417    Tue Sep 01 21:46:56 +0000 2015
3276255125    True Equality    ernestsgantt: BeyHiveInFrance: 9_A_6:
ernestsg...    3    2
3    3    638830424563716097    Tue Sep 01 21:46:56 +0000 2015
3276255125    True Equality    ernestsgantt: BeyHiveInFrance:
PhuketDailyNews...    3    3
```

```
4    4    638830422256816132        Tue Sep 01 21:46:56 +0000 2015
3276255125    True Equality          ernestsgantt: elsahel12: 9_A_6:
dreamintention...    3    4
5    5    638830420159655936        Tue Sep 01 21:46:55 +0000 2015
3276255125    True Equality          ernestsgantt: BeyHiveInFrance:
PhuketDailyNews...    3    5
7    7    638830418330980352        Tue Sep 01 21:46:55 +0000 2015
3276255125    True Equality          ernestsgantt: elsahel12: 9_A_6:
dreamintention...    3    7
8    8    638830397648822272        Tue Sep 01 21:46:50 +0000 2015
3276255125    True Equality          ernestsgantt: BeyHiveInFrance:
PhuketDailyNews...    3    8
9    9    638830395375529984        Tue Sep 01 21:46:49 +0000 2015
3276255125    True Equality          ernestsgantt: elsahel12: 9_A_6:
dreamintention...    3    9
10    10    638830392389177344        Tue Sep 01 21:46:49 +0000 2015
3276255125    True Equality          ernestsgantt: BeyHiveInFrance:
PhuketDailyNews...    3    10
In [83]:
```

```
pddf_with_cluster[pddf_with_cluster['_1'] == 4].head(10)
```

```
Out[83]:
    Unnamed: 0    id    created_at    user_id    user_name    tweet_text    _1
_2
1361    882    642648214454317056    Sat Sep 12 10:37:28 +0000 2015
27415756    Raymond Enisuoh    LA Chosen For US 2024 Olympic Bid -
LA2016 See...    4    1361
1363    885    642647848744583168    Sat Sep 12 10:36:01 +0000 2015
27415756    Raymond Enisuoh    Prison See: https://t.co/x3EKAExeFi … … …
… … ...    4    1363
5412    11    640480770369286144    Sun Sep 06 11:04:49 +0000 2015
3242403023    Donald Trump 2016    " igiboooy! @ Starbucks https://t.
co/97wdL...    4    5412
5428    27    640477140660518912    Sun Sep 06 10:50:24 +0000 2015
3242403023    Donald Trump 2016    " @ Starbucks https://t.co/
wsEYFIefk7 " - D...    4    5428
5455    61    640469542272110592    Sun Sep 06 10:20:12 +0000 2015
3242403023    Donald Trump 2016    " starbucks @ Starbucks Mam Plaza
https://t.co...    4    5455
5456    62    640469541370372096    Sun Sep 06 10:20:12 +0000 2015
3242403023    Donald Trump 2016    " Aaahhh the pumpkin spice latte is
back, fall...    4    5456
5457    63    640469539524898817    Sun Sep 06 10:20:12 +0000 2015
3242403023    Donald Trump 2016    " RT kayyleighferry: Oh my goddd
Harry Potter ...    4    5457
5458    64    640469537176031232    Sun Sep 06 10:20:11 +0000 2015
3242403023    Donald Trump 2016    " Starbucks https://t.co/3xYYXlwNkf
" - Donald...    4    5458
```

```
5459   65    640469536119070720    Sun Sep 06 10:20:11 +0000 2015
3242403023   Donald Trump 2016     " A Starbucks is under construction
in my neig...   4    5459
5460   66    640469530435813376    Sun Sep 06 10:20:10 +0000 2015
3242403023   Donald Trump 2016     " Babam starbucks'tan fotogtaf atıyor
bende du...   4    5460
```

We map the 5 clusters with some sample tweets. Cluster 0 is about Spark. Cluster 1 is about Python. Cluster 2 is about Lady Gaga. Cluster 3 is about Thailand's Phuket News. Cluster 4 is about Donald Trump.

Building machine learning pipelines

We want to compose the feature extraction, preparatory activities, training, testing, and prediction activities while optimizing the best tuning parameter to get the best performing model.

The following tweet captures perfectly in five lines of code a powerful machine learning Pipeline implemented in Spark MLlib:

The Spark ML pipeline is inspired by Python's Scikit-Learn and creates a succinct, declarative statement of the successive transformations to the data in order to quickly deliver a tunable model.

Summary

In this chapter, we got an overview of Spark MLlib's ever-expanding library of algorithms Spark MLlib. We discussed supervised and unsupervised learning, recommender systems, optimization, and feature extraction algorithms. We then put the harvested data from Twitter into the machine learning process, algorithms, and evaluation to derive insights from the data. We put the Twitter-harvested dataset through a Python Scikit-Learn and Spark MLlib K-means clustering in order to segregate the tweets relevant to *Apache Spark*. We also evaluated the performance of the model.

This gets us ready for the next chapter, which will cover Streaming Analytics using Spark. Let's jump right in.

5
Streaming Live Data with Spark

In this chapter, we will focus on live streaming data flowing into Spark and processing it. So far, we have discussed machine learning and data mining with batch processing. We are now looking at processing continuously flowing data and detecting facts and patterns on the fly. We are navigating from a lake to a river.

We will first investigate the challenges arising from such a dynamic and ever changing environment. After laying the grounds on the prerequisite of a streaming application, we will investigate various implementations using live sources of data such as TCP sockets to the Twitter firehose and put in place a low latency, high throughput, and scalable data pipeline combining Spark, Kafka and Flume.

In this chapter, we will cover the following points:

- Analyzing a streaming application's architectural challenges, constraints, and requirements
- Processing live data from a TCP socket with Spark Streaming
- Connecting to the Twitter firehose directly to parse tweets in quasi real time
- Establishing a reliable, fault tolerant, scalable, high throughput, low latency integrated application using Spark, Kafka, and Flume
- Closing remarks on Lambda and Kappa architecture paradigms

Laying the foundations of streaming architecture

As customary, let's first go back to our original drawing of the data-intensive apps architecture blueprint and highlight the Spark Streaming module that will be the topic of interest.

The following diagram sets the context by highlighting the Spark Streaming module and interactions with Spark SQL and Spark MLlib within the overall data-intensive apps framework.

Data flows from stock market time series, enterprise transactions, interactions, events, web traffic, click streams, and sensors. All events are time-stamped data and urgent. This is the case for fraud detection and prevention, mobile cross-sell and upsell, or traffic alerts. Those streams of data require immediate processing for monitoring purposes, such as detecting anomalies, outliers, spam, fraud, and intrusion; and also for providing basic statistics, insights, trends, and recommendations. In some cases, the summarized aggregated information is sufficient to be stored for later usage. From an architecture paradigm perspective, we are moving from a service-oriented architecture to an event-driven architecture.

Two models emerge for processing streams of data:

- Processing one record at a time as they come in. We do not buffer the incoming records in a container before processing them. This is the case of Twitter's Storm, Yahoo's S4, and Google's MillWheel.
- Micro-batching or batch computations on small intervals as performed by Spark Streaming and Storm Trident. In this case, we buffer the incoming records in a container according to the time window prescribed in the micro-batching settings.

Spark Streaming has often been compared against Storm. They are two different models of streaming data. Spark Streaming is based on micro-batching. Storm is based on processing records as they come in. Storm also offers a micro-batching option, with its Storm Trident option.

The driving factor in a streaming application is latency. Latency varies from the milliseconds range in the case of **RPC** (short for **Remote Procedure Call**) to several seconds or minutes for micro batching solution such as Spark Streaming.

RPC allows synchronous operations between the requesting programs waiting for the results from the remote server's procedure. Threads allow concurrency of multiple RPC calls to the server.

An example of software implementing a distributed RPC model is Apache Storm.

Storm implements stateless sub millisecond latency processing of unbounded tuples using topologies or directed acyclic graphs combining spouts as source of data streams and bolts for operations such as filter, join, aggregation, and transformation. Storm also implements a higher level abstraction called **Trident** which, similarly to Spark, processes data streams in micro batches.

So, looking at the latency continuum, from sub millisecond to second, Storm is a good candidate. For seconds to minutes scale, Spark Streaming and Storm Trident are excellent fits. For several minutes onward, Spark and a NoSQL database such as Cassandra or HBase are adequate solutions. For ranges beyond the hour and with high volume of data, Hadoop is the ideal contender.

Although throughput is correlated to latency, it is not a simple inversely linear relationship. If processing a message takes 2 ms, which determines the latency, then one would assume the throughput is limited to 500 messages per sec. Batching messages allows for higher throughput if we allow our messages to be buffered for 8 ms more. With a latency of 10 ms, the system can buffer up to 10,000 messages. For a bearable increase in latency, we have substantially increased throughput. This is the magic of micro-batching that Spark Streaming exploits.

Spark Streaming inner working

The Spark Streaming architecture leverages the Spark core architecture. It overlays on the **SparkContext** a **StreamingContext** as the entry point to the Stream functionality. The Cluster Manager will dedicate at least one worker node as Receiver, which will be an executor with a *long task* to process the incoming stream. The Executor creates Discretized Streams or DStreams from input data stream and replicates by default, the DStream to the cache of another worker. One receiver serves one input data stream. Multiple receivers improve parallelism and generate multiple DStreams that Spark can unite or join Resilient Distributed Datasets (RDD).

The following diagram gives an overview of the inner working of Spark Streaming. The client interacts with the Spark Cluster via the cluster manager, while Spark Streaming has a dedicated worker with a long running task ingesting the input data stream and transforming it into discretized streams or DStreams. The data is collected, buffered and replicated by a receiver and then pushed to a stream of RDDs.

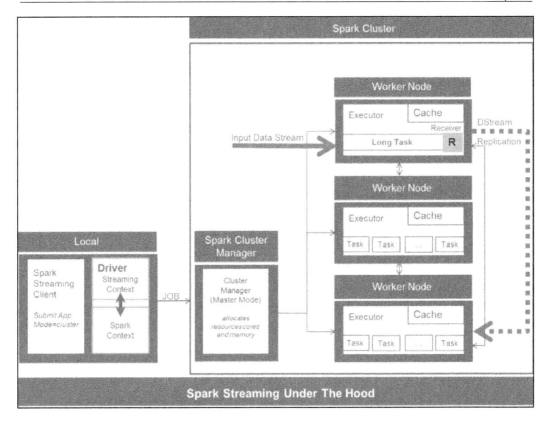

Spark receivers can ingest data from many sources. Core input sources range from TCP socket and HDFS/Amazon S3 to Akka Actors. Additional sources include Apache Kafka, Apache Flume, Amazon Kinesis, ZeroMQ, Twitter, and custom or user-defined receivers.

We distinguish between reliable resources that acknowledges receipt of data to the source and replication for possible resend, versus unreliable receivers who do not acknowledge receipt of the message. Spark scales out in terms of the number of workers, partition and receivers.

The following diagram gives an overview of Spark Streaming with the possible sources and the persistence options:

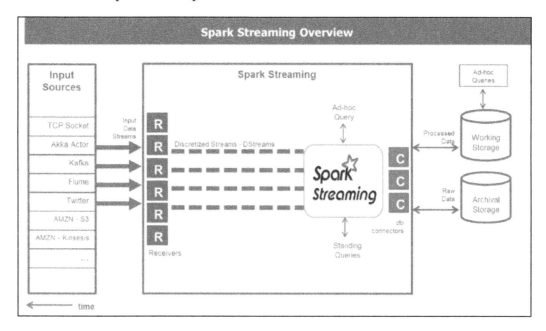

Going under the hood of Spark Streaming

Spark Streaming is composed of Receivers and powered by Discretized Streams and Spark Connectors for persistence.

As for Spark Core, the essential data structure is the RDD, the fundamental programming abstraction for Spark Streaming is the Discretized Stream or DStream.

The following diagram illustrates the Discretized Streams as continuous sequences of RDDs. The batch intervals of DStream are configurable.

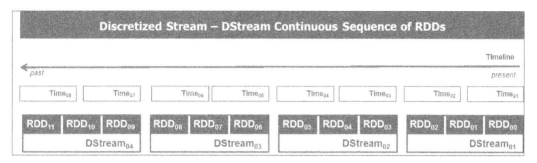

DStreams snapshots the incoming data in batch intervals. Those time steps typically range from 500 ms to several seconds. The underlying structure of a DStream is an RDD.

A DStream is essentially a continuous sequence of RDDs. This is powerful as it allows us to leverage from Spark Streaming all the traditional functions, transformations and actions available in Spark Core and allows us to dialogue with Spark SQL, performing SQL queries on incoming streams of data and Spark MLlib. Transformations similar to those on generic and key-value pair RDDs are applicable. The DStreams benefit from the inner RDDs lineage and fault tolerance. Additional transformation and output operations exist for discretized stream operations. Most generic operations on DStream are **transform** and **foreachRDD**.

The following diagram gives an overview of the lifecycle of DStreams. From creation of the micro-batches of messages materialized to RDDs on which `transformation` function and actions that trigger Spark jobs are applied. Breaking down the steps illustrated in the diagram, we read the diagram top down:

1. In the Input Stream, the incoming messages are buffered in a container according to the time window allocated for the micro-batching.

2. In the discretized stream step, the buffered micro-batches are transformed as DStream RDDs.

3. The Mapped DStream step is obtained by applying a transformation function to the original DStream. These first three steps constitute the transformation of the original data received in predefined time windows. As the underlying data structure is the RDD, we conserve the data lineage of the transformations.

4. The final step is an action on the RDD. It triggers the Spark job.

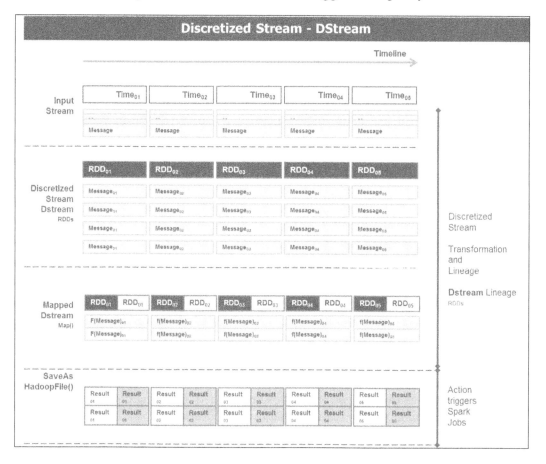

Transformation can be stateless or stateful. *Stateless* means that no state is maintained by the program, while *stateful* means the program keeps a state, in which case previous transactions are remembered and may affect the current transaction. A stateful operation modifies or requires some state of the system, and a stateless operation does not.

Stateless transformations process each batch in a DStream at a time. Stateful transformations process multiple batches to obtain results. Stateful transformations require the checkpoint directory to be configured. Check pointing is the main mechanism for fault tolerance in Spark Streaming to periodically save data and metadata about an application.

There are two types of stateful transformations for Spark Streaming: updateStateByKey and windowed transformations.

`updateStateByKey` are transformations that maintain state for each key in a stream of Pair RDDs. It returns a new *state* DStream where the state for each key is updated by applying the given function on the previous state of the key and the new values of each key. An example would be a running count of given hashtags in a stream of tweets.

Windowed transformations are carried over multiple batches in a sliding window. A window has a defined length or duration specified in time units. It must be a multiple of a DStream batch interval. It defines how many batches are included in a windowed transformation.

A window has a sliding interval or sliding duration specified in time units. It must be a multiple of a DStream batch interval. It defines how many batches to slide a window or how frequently to compute a windowed transformation.

The following schema depicts the windowing operation on DStreams to derive window DStreams with a given length and sliding interval:

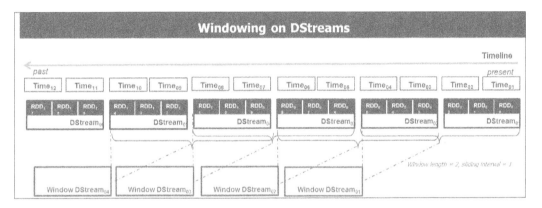

A sample function is `countByWindow (windowLength, slideInterval)`. It returns a new DStream in which each RDD has a single element generated by counting the number of elements in a sliding window over this DStream. An illustration in this case would be a running count of given hashtags in a stream of tweets every 60 seconds. The window time frame is specified.

Minute scale window length is reasonable. Hour scale window length is not recommended as it is compute and memory intensive. It would be more convenient to aggregate the data in a database such as Cassandra or HBase.

Windowed transformations compute results based on window length and window slide interval. Spark performance is primarily affected by on window length, window slide interval, and persistence.

Building in fault tolerance

Real-time stream processing systems must be operational 24/7. They need to be resilient to all sorts of failures in the system. Spark and its RDD abstraction are designed to seamlessly handle failures of any worker nodes in the cluster.

Main Spark Streaming fault tolerance mechanisms are check pointing, automatic driver restart, and automatic failover. Spark enables recovery from driver failure using check pointing, which preserves the application state.

Write ahead logs, reliable receivers, and file streams guarantees zero data loss as of Spark Version 1.2. Write ahead logs represent a fault tolerant storage for received data.

Failures require recomputing results. DStream operations have exactly-one semantics. Transformations can be recomputed multiple times but will yield the same result. DStream output operations have at least once semantics. Output operations may be executed multiple times.

Processing live data with TCP sockets

As a stepping stone to the overall understanding of streaming operations, we will first experiment with TCP socket. TCP socket establishes two-way communication between client and server, and it can exchange data through the established connection. WebSocket connections are long lived, unlike typical HTTP connections. HTTP is not meant to keep an open connection from the server to push continuously data to the web browsers. Most web applications hence resorted to long polling via frequent **Asynchronous JavaScript** (**AJAX**) and XML requests. WebSockets, standardized and implemented in HTML5, are moving beyond web browsers and are becoming a cross-platform standard for real-time communication between client and server.

Setting up TCP sockets

We create a TCP Socket Server by running `netcat`, a small utility found in most Linux systems, as a data server with the command `> nc -lk 9999`, where `9999` is the port where we are sending data:

```
#
# Socket Server
#
an@an-VB:~$ nc -lk 9999
```

```
hello world
how are you
hello  world
cool it works
```

Once netcat is running, we will open a second console with our Spark Streaming client to receive the data and process. As soon as the Spark Streaming client console is listening, we start typing the words to be processed, that is, `hello world`.

Processing live data

We will be using the example program provided in the Spark bundle for Spark Streaming called `network_wordcount.py`. It can be found on the GitHub repository under `https://github.com/apache/spark/blob/master/examples/src/main/python/streaming/network_wordcount.py`. The code is as follows:

```python
"""
 Counts words in UTF8 encoded, '\n' delimited text received from the
network every second.
 Usage: network_wordcount.py <hostname> <port>
   <hostname> and <port> describe the TCP server that Spark Streaming
would connect to receive data.
 To run this on your local machine, you need to first run a Netcat
server
    `$ nc -lk 9999`
 and then run the example
    `$ bin/spark-submit examples/src/main/python/streaming/network_
wordcount.py localhost 9999`
"""
from __future__ import print_function

import sys

from pyspark import SparkContext
from pyspark.streaming import StreamingContext

if __name__ == "__main__":
    if len(sys.argv) != 3:
        print("Usage: network_wordcount.py <hostname> <port>",
file=sys.stderr)
        exit(-1)
    sc = SparkContext(appName="PythonStreamingNetworkWordCount")
    ssc = StreamingContext(sc, 1)
```

```
lines = ssc.socketTextStream(sys.argv[1], int(sys.argv[2]))
counts = lines.flatMap(lambda line: line.split(" "))\
              .map(lambda word: (word, 1))\
              .reduceByKey(lambda a, b: a+b)
counts.pprint()

ssc.start()
ssc.awaitTermination()
```

Here, we explain the steps of the program:

1. The code first initializes a Spark Streaming Context with the command:

   `ssc = StreamingContext(sc, 1)`

2. Next, the streaming computation is set up.

3. One or more DStream objects that receive data are defined to connect to localhost or `127.0.0.1` on `port 9999`:

   `stream = ssc.socketTextStream("127.0.0.1", 9999)`

4. The DStream computation is defined: transformations and output operations:

   ```
   stream.map(x: lambda (x,1))
   .reduce(a+b)
   .print()
   ```

5. Computation is started:

   `ssc.start()`

6. Program termination is pending manual or error processing completion:

   `ssc.awaitTermination()`

7. Manual completion is an option when a completion condition is known:

   `ssc.stop()`

We can monitor the Spark Streaming application by visiting the Spark monitoring home page at `localhost:4040`.

Here's the result of running the program and feeding the words on the `netcat` 4server console:

```
#
# Socket Client
# an@an-VB:~/spark/spark-1.5.0-bin-hadoop2.6$ ./bin/spark-submit
examples/src/main/python/streaming/network_wordcount.py localhost 9999
```

Run the Spark Streaming `network_count` program by connecting to the socket localhost on `port 9999`:

```
an@an-VB:~/spark/spark-1.5.0-bin-hadoop2.6$ ./bin/spark-submit examples/
src/main/python/streaming/network_wordcount.py localhost 9999
-------------------------------------------
Time: 2015-10-18 20:06:06
-------------------------------------------
(u'world', 1)
(u'hello', 1)


-------------------------------------------
Time: 2015-10-18 20:06:07
-------------------------------------------
. . .
-------------------------------------------
Time: 2015-10-18 20:06:17
-------------------------------------------
(u'you', 1)
(u'how', 1)
(u'are', 1)


-------------------------------------------
Time: 2015-10-18 20:06:18
-------------------------------------------


. . .

-------------------------------------------
Time: 2015-10-18 20:06:26
-------------------------------------------
(u'', 1)
(u'world', 1)
(u'hello', 1)
```

```
-------------------------------------------
Time: 2015-10-18 20:06:27
-------------------------------------------
. . .
-------------------------------------------
Time: 2015-10-18 20:06:37
-------------------------------------------
(u'works', 1)
(u'it', 1)
(u'cool', 1)


-------------------------------------------
Time: 2015-10-18 20:06:38
-------------------------------------------
```

Thus, we have established connection through the socket on `port 9999`, streamed the data sent by the `netcat` server, and performed a word count on the messages sent.

Manipulating Twitter data in real time

Twitter offers two APIs. One search API that essentially allows us to retrieve past tweets based on search terms. This is how we have been collecting our data from Twitter in the previous chapters of the book. Interestingly, for our current purpose, Twitter offers a live streaming API which allows to ingest tweets as they are emitted in the blogosphere.

Processing Tweets in real time from the Twitter firehose

The following program connects to the Twitter firehose and processes the incoming tweets to exclude deleted or invalid tweets and parses on the fly only the relevant ones to extract `screen name`, the actual tweet, or `tweet text`, `retweet` count, `geo-location` information. The processed tweets are gathered into an RDD Queue by Spark Streaming and then displayed on the console at a one-second interval:

```
"""
Twitter Streaming API Spark Streaming into an RDD-Queue to process
tweets live
```

Create a queue of RDDs that will be mapped/reduced one at a time in 1 second intervals.

```
To run this example use
    '$ bin/spark-submit examples/AN_Spark/AN_Spark_Code/s07_
twitterstreaming.py'

"""
#
import time
from pyspark import SparkContext
from pyspark.streaming import StreamingContext
import twitter
import dateutil.parser
import json


# Connecting Streaming Twitter with Streaming Spark via Queue
class Tweet(dict):
    def __init__(self, tweet_in):
        super(Tweet, self).__init__(self)
        if tweet_in and 'delete' not in tweet_in:
            self['timestamp'] = dateutil.parser.parse(tweet_
in[u'created_at']
                                ).replace(tzinfo=None).isoformat()
            self['text'] = tweet_in['text'].encode('utf-8')
            #self['text'] = tweet_in['text']
            self['hashtags'] = [x['text'].encode('utf-8') for x in
tweet_in['entities']['hashtags']]
            #self['hashtags'] = [x['text'] for x in tweet_
in['entities']['hashtags']]
            self['geo'] = tweet_in['geo']['coordinates'] if tweet_
in['geo'] else None
            self['id'] = tweet_in['id']
            self['screen_name'] = tweet_in['user']['screen_name'].
encode('utf-8')
            #self['screen_name'] = tweet_in['user']['screen_name']
            self['user_id'] = tweet_in['user']['id']


def connect_twitter():
    twitter_stream = twitter.TwitterStream(auth=twitter.OAuth(
        token = "get_your_own_credentials",
        token_secret = "get_your_own_credentials",
        consumer_key = "get_your_own_credentials",
        consumer_secret = "get_your_own_credentials"))
```

```
        return twitter_stream

    def get_next_tweet(twitter_stream):
        stream = twitter_stream.statuses.sample(block=True)
        tweet_in = None
        while not tweet_in or 'delete' in tweet_in:
            tweet_in = stream.next()
            tweet_parsed = Tweet(tweet_in)
        return json.dumps(tweet_parsed)

    def process_rdd_queue(twitter_stream):
        # Create the queue through which RDDs can be pushed to
        # a QueueInputDStream
        rddQueue = []
        for i in range(3):
            rddQueue += [ssc.sparkContext.parallelize([get_next_
tweet(twitter_stream)], 5)]

        lines = ssc.queueStream(rddQueue)
        lines.pprint()

    if __name__ == "__main__":
        sc = SparkContext(appName="PythonStreamingQueueStream")
        ssc = StreamingContext(sc, 1)

        # Instantiate the twitter_stream
        twitter_stream = connect_twitter()
        # Get RDD queue of the streams json or parsed
        process_rdd_queue(twitter_stream)

        ssc.start()
        time.sleep(2)
        ssc.stop(stopSparkContext=True, stopGraceFully=True)
```

When we run this program, it delivers the following output:

```
an@an-VB:~/spark/spark-1.5.0-bin-hadoop2.6$ bin/spark-submit examples/
AN_Spark/AN_Spark_Code/s07_twitterstreaming.py
-------------------------------------------
Time: 2015-11-03 21:53:14
-------------------------------------------
```

{"user_id": 3242732207, "screen_name": "cypuqygoducu", "timestamp": "2015-11-03T20:53:04", "hashtags": [], "text": "RT @VIralBuzzNewss: Our Distinctive Edition Holiday break Challenge Is In this article! Hooray!... - https://t.co/9d8wumrd5v https://t.co/\u2026", "geo": null, "id": 661647303678259200}

```
--------------------------------------------
```

Time: 2015-11-03 21:53:15

```
--------------------------------------------
```

{"user_id": 352673159, "screen_name": "melly_boo_orig", "timestamp": "2015-11-03T20:53:05", "hashtags": ["eminem"], "text": "#eminem https://t.co/GlEjPJnwxy", "geo": null, "id": 661647307847409668}

```
--------------------------------------------
```

Time: 2015-11-03 21:53:16

```
--------------------------------------------
```

{"user_id": 500620889, "screen_name": "NBAtheist", "timestamp": "2015-11-03T20:53:06", "hashtags": ["tehInterwebbies", "Nutters"], "text": "See? That didn't take long or any actual effort. This is #tehInterwebbies ... #Nutters Abound! https://t.co/QS8gLStYFO", "geo": null, "id": 661647312062709761}

So, we got an example of streaming tweets with Spark and processing them on the fly.

Building a reliable and scalable streaming app

Ingesting data is the process of acquiring data from various sources and storing it for processing immediately or at a later stage. Data consuming systems are dispersed and can be physically and architecturally far from the sources. Data ingestion is often implemented manually with scripts and rudimentary automation. It actually calls for higher level frameworks like Flume and Kafka.

The challenges of data ingestion arise from the fact that the sources are physically spread out and are transient which makes the integration brittle. Data production is continuous for weather, traffic, social media, network activity, shop floor sensors, security, and surveillance. Ever increasing data volumes and rates coupled with ever changing data structure and semantics makes data ingestion ad hoc and error prone.

The aim is to become more agile, reliable, and scalable. Agility, reliability, and scalability of the data ingestion determine the overall health of the pipeline. Agility means integrating new sources as they arise and incorporating changes to existing sources as needed. In order to ensure safety and reliability, we need to protect the infrastructure against data loss and downstream applications from silent data corruption at ingress. Scalability avoids ingest bottlenecks while keeping cost tractable.

Ingest Mode	Description	Example
Manual or Scripted	File copy using command line interface or GUI interface	HDFS Client, Cloudera Hue
Batch Data Transport	Bulk data transport using tools	DistCp, Sqoop
Micro Batch	Transport of small batches of data	Sqoop, Sqoop2 Storm
Pipelining	Flow like transport of event streams	Flume Scribe
Message Queue	Publish Subscribe message bus of events	Kafka, Kinesis

In order to enable an event-driven business that is able to ingest multiple streams of data, process it in flight, and make sense of it all to get to rapid decisions, the key driver is the Unified Log.

A Unified Log is a centralized enterprise structured log available for real-time subscription. All the organization's data is put in a central log for subscription. Records are numbered beginning with zero in the order that they are written. It is also known as a commit log or journal. The concept of the *Unified Log* is the central tenet of the Kappa architecture.

The properties of the Unified Log are as follows:

- **Unified**: There is a single deployment for the entire organization
- **Append only**: Events are immutable and are appended
- **Ordered**: Each event has a unique offset within a shard
- **Distributed**: For fault tolerance purpose, the Unified Log is distributed redundantly on a cluster of computers
- **Fast**: The systems ingests thousands of messages per second

Setting up Kafka

In order to isolate downstream particular consumption of data from the vagaries of upstream emission of data, we need to decouple the providers of data from the receivers or consumers of data. As they are living in two different worlds with different cycles and constraints, Kafka decouples the data pipelines.

Apache Kafka is a distributed publish subscribe messaging system rethought as a distributed commit log. The messages are stored by topic.

Apache Kafka has the following properties. It supports:

- High throughput for high volume of events feeds
- Real-time processing of new and derived feeds
- Large data backlogs and persistence for offline consumption
- Low latency as enterprise wide messaging system
- Fault tolerance thanks to its distributed nature

Messages are stored in partition with a unique sequential ID called `offset`. Consumers track their pointers via tuple of (`offset`, `partition`, `topic`).

Let's dive deeper in the anatomy of Kafka.

Kafka has essentially three components: *producers*, *consumers* and *brokers*. Producers push and write data to brokers. Consumers pull and read data from brokers. Brokers do not push messages to consumers. Consumers pull message from brokers. The setup is distributed and coordinated by Apache Zookeeper.

The brokers manage and store the data in topics. Topics are split in replicated partitions. The data is persisted in the broker, but not removed upon consumption, but until retention period. If a consumer fails, it can always go back to the broker to fetch the data.

Kafka requires Apache ZooKeeper. ZooKeeper is a high-performance coordination service for distributed applications. It centrally manages configuration, registry or naming service, group membership, lock, and synchronization for coordination between servers. It provides a hierarchical namespace with metadata, monitoring statistics, and state of the cluster. ZooKeeper can introduce brokers and consumers on the fly and then rebalances the cluster.

Kafka producers do not need ZooKeeper. Kafka brokers use ZooKeeper to provide general state information as well elect leader in case of failure. Kafka consumers use ZooKeeper to track message offset. Newer versions of Kafka will save the consumers to go through ZooKeeper and can retrieve the Kafka special topics information. Kafka provides automatic load balancing for producers.

The following diagram gives an overview of the Kafka setup:

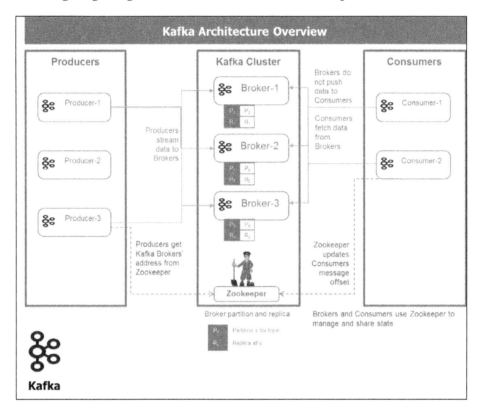

Installing and testing Kafka

We will download the Apache Kafka binaries from the dedicated web page at `http://kafka.apache.org/downloads.html` and install the software in our machine using the following steps:

1. Download the code.

2. Download the 0.8.2.0 release and `un-tar` it:

   ```
   > tar -xzf kafka_2.10-0.8.2.0.tgz
   > cd kafka_2.10-0.8.2.0
   ```

3. Start `zooeeper`. Kafka uses ZooKeeper so we need to first start a ZooKeeper server. We will use the convenience script packaged with Kafka to get a single-node ZooKeeper instance.

```
> bin/zookeeper-server-start.sh config/zookeeper.properties

an@an-VB:~/kafka/kafka_2.10-0.8.2.0$ bin/zookeeper-server-start.sh
config/zookeeper.properties


[2015-10-31 22:49:14,808] INFO Reading configuration from:
config/zookeeper.properties (org.apache.zookeeper.server.quorum.
QuorumPeerConfig)

[2015-10-31 22:49:14,816] INFO autopurge.snapRetainCount set to 3
(org.apache.zookeeper.server.DatadirCleanupManager)...
```

4. Now launch the Kafka server:

```
> bin/kafka-server-start.sh config/server.properties


an@an-VB:~/kafka/kafka_2.10-0.8.2.0$ bin/kafka-server-start.sh
config/server.properties

[2015-10-31 22:52:04,643] INFO Verifying properties (kafka.utils.
VerifiableProperties)

[2015-10-31 22:52:04,714] INFO Property broker.id is overridden to
0 (kafka.utils.VerifiableProperties)

[2015-10-31 22:52:04,715] INFO Property log.cleaner.enable is
overridden to false (kafka.utils.VerifiableProperties)

[2015-10-31 22:52:04,715] INFO Property log.dirs is overridden to
/tmp/kafka-logs (kafka.utils.VerifiableProperties) [2013-04-22
15:01:47,051] INFO Property socket.send.buffer.bytes is overridden
to 1048576 (kafka.utils.VerifiableProperties)
```

5. Create a topic. Let's create a topic named test with a single partition and only one replica:

```
> bin/kafka-topics.sh --create --zookeeper localhost:2181
--replication-factor 1 --partitions 1 --topic test
```

6. We can now see that topic if we run the `list` topic command:

```
> bin/kafka-topics.sh --list --zookeeper localhost:2181

Test

an@an-VB:~/kafka/kafka_2.10-0.8.2.0$ bin/kafka-topics.sh --create
--zookeeper localhost:2181 --replication-factor 1 --partitions 1
--topic test

Created topic "test".
```

```
an@an-VB:~/kafka/kafka_2.10-0.8.2.0$ bin/kafka-topics.sh --list
--zookeeper localhost:2181

test
```

7. Check the Kafka installation by creating a producer and consumer. We first launch a `producer` and type a message in the console:

```
an@an-VB:~/kafka/kafka_2.10-0.8.2.0$ bin/kafka-console-producer.sh
--broker-list localhost:9092 --topic test

[2015-10-31 22:54:43,698] WARN Property topic is not valid (kafka.
utils.VerifiableProperties)

This is a message

This is another message
```

8. We then launch a consumer to check that we receive the message:

```
an@an-VB:~$ cd kafka/

an@an-VB:~/kafka$ cd kafka_2.10-0.8.2.0/

an@an-VB:~/kafka/kafka_2.10-0.8.2.0$ bin/kafka-console-consumer.sh
--zookeeper localhost:2181 --topic test --from-beginning

This is a message

This is another message
```

The messages were appropriately received by the consumer:

1. Check Kafka and Spark Streaming consumer. We will be using the Spark Streaming Kafka word count example provided in the Spark bundle. A word of caution: we have to bind the Kafka packages, `--packages org.apache.spark:spark-streaming-kafka_2.10:1.5.0`, when we submit the Spark job. The command is as follows:

```
./bin/spark-submit --packages org.apache.spark:spark-streaming-
kafka_2.10:1.5.0 \ examples/src/main/python/streaming/kafka_
wordcount.py \

localhost:2181 test
```

2. When we launch the Spark Streaming word count program with Kafka, we get the following output:

```
an@an-VB:~/spark/spark-1.5.0-bin-hadoop2.6$ ./bin/spark-submit
--packages org.apache.spark:spark-streaming-kafka_2.10:1.5.0
examples/src/main/python/streaming/kafka_wordcount.py
localhost:2181 test


-------------------------------------------

Time: 2015-10-31 23:46:33
```

```
-----------------------------------------------
(u'', 1)
(u'from', 2)
(u'Hello', 2)
(u'Kafka', 2)


-----------------------------------------------
Time: 2015-10-31 23:46:34
-----------------------------------------------


-----------------------------------------------
Time: 2015-10-31 23:46:35
-----------------------------------------------
```

3. Install the Kafka Python driver in order to be able to programmatically develop Producers and Consumers and interact with Kafka and Spark using Python. We will use the road-tested library from David Arthur, aka, Mumrah on GitHub (https://github.com/mumrah). We can pip install it as follows:

```
> pip install kafka-python
an@an-VB:~$ pip install kafka-python
Collecting kafka-python
  Downloading kafka-python-0.9.4.tar.gz (63kB)
...
Successfully installed kafka-python-0.9.4
```

Developing producers

The following program creates a Simple Kafka Producer that will emit the message *this is a message sent from the Kafka producer:* five times, followed by a time stamp every second:

```
#
# kafka producer
#
#
import time
from kafka.common import LeaderNotAvailableError
from kafka.client import KafkaClient
from kafka.producer import SimpleProducer
```

```
from datetime import datetime

def print_response(response=None):
    if response:
        print('Error: {0}'.format(response[0].error))
        print('Offset: {0}'.format(response[0].offset))

def main():
    kafka = KafkaClient("localhost:9092")
    producer = SimpleProducer(kafka)
    try:
        time.sleep(5)
        topic = 'test'
        for i in range(5):
            time.sleep(1)
            msg = 'This is a message sent from the kafka producer: ' \
                    + str(datetime.now().time()) + ' -- '\
                    + str(datetime.now().strftime("%A, %d %B %Y
                        %I:%M%p"))
            print_response(producer.send_messages(topic, msg))
    except LeaderNotAvailableError:
        # https://github.com/mumrah/kafka-python/issues/249
        time.sleep(1)
        print_response(producer.send_messages(topic, msg))

    kafka.close()

if __name__ == "__main__":
    main()
```

When we run this program, the following output is generated:

```
an@an-VB:~/spark/spark-1.5.0-bin-hadoop2.6/examples/AN_Spark/AN_Spark_
Code$ python s08_kafka_producer_01.py
Error: 0
Offset: 13
Error: 0
Offset: 14
Error: 0
Offset: 15
Error: 0
Offset: 16
```

```
Error: 0
```

```
Offset: 17
```

```
an@an-VB:~/spark/spark-1.5.0-bin-hadoop2.6/examples/AN_Spark/AN_Spark_
Code$
```

It tells us there were no errors and gives the offset of the messages given by the Kafka broker.

Developing consumers

To fetch the messages from the Kafka brokers, we develop a Kafka consumer:

```
# kafka consumer
# consumes messages from "test" topic and writes them to console.
#
from kafka.client import KafkaClient
from kafka.consumer import SimpleConsumer

def main():
  kafka = KafkaClient("localhost:9092")
  print("Consumer established connection to kafka")
  consumer = SimpleConsumer(kafka, "my-group", "test")
  for message in consumer:
    # This will wait and print messages as they become available
    print(message)

if __name__ == "__main__":
    main()
```

When we run this program, we effectively confirm that the consumer received all the messages:

```
an@an-VB:~$ cd ~/spark/spark-1.5.0-bin-hadoop2.6/examples/AN_Spark/AN_
Spark_Code/
```

```
an@an-VB:~/spark/spark-1.5.0-bin-hadoop2.6/examples/AN_Spark/AN_Spark_
Code$ python s08_kafka_consumer_01.py
```

```
Consumer established connection to kafka
```

```
OffsetAndMessage(offset=13, message=Message(magic=0, attributes=0,
key=None, value='This is a message sent from the kafka producer:
11:50:17.867309Sunday, 01 November 2015 11:50AM'))
```

```
...
```

```
OffsetAndMessage(offset=17, message=Message(magic=0, attributes=0,
key=None, value='This is a message sent from the kafka producer:
11:50:22.051423Sunday, 01 November 2015 11:50AM'))
```

Developing a Spark Streaming consumer for Kafka

Based on the example code provided in the Spark Streaming bundle, we will create a Spark Streaming consumer for Kafka and perform a word count on the messages stored with the brokers:

```
#
# Kafka Spark Streaming Consumer
#
from __future__ import print_function

import sys

from pyspark import SparkContext
from pyspark.streaming import StreamingContext
from pyspark.streaming.kafka import KafkaUtils

if __name__ == "__main__":
    if len(sys.argv) != 3:
        print("Usage: kafka_spark_consumer_01.py <zk> <topic>",
file=sys.stderr)
        exit(-1)

    sc = SparkContext(appName="PythonStreamingKafkaWordCount")
    ssc = StreamingContext(sc, 1)

    zkQuorum, topic = sys.argv[1:]
    kvs = KafkaUtils.createStream(ssc, zkQuorum, "spark-streaming-
consumer", {topic: 1})
    lines = kvs.map(lambda x: x[1])
    counts = lines.flatMap(lambda line: line.split(" ")) \
        .map(lambda word: (word, 1)) \
        .reduceByKey(lambda a, b: a+b)
    counts.pprint()

    ssc.start()
    ssc.awaitTermination()
```

Run this program with the following Spark submit command:

```
./bin/spark-submit --packages org.apache.spark:spark-streaming-
kafka_2.10:1.5.0 examples/AN_Spark/AN_Spark_Code/s08_kafka_spark_
consumer_01.py localhost:2181 test
```

We get the following output:

```
an@an-VB:~$ cd spark/spark-1.5.0-bin-hadoop2.6/
an@an-VB:~/spark/spark-1.5.0-bin-hadoop2.6$ ./bin/spark-submit \
>       --packages org.apache.spark:spark-streaming-kafka_2.10:1.5.0 \
>       examples/AN_Spark/AN_Spark_Code/s08_kafka_spark_consumer_01.py
localhost:2181 test
...
:: retrieving :: org.apache.spark#spark-submit-parent
  confs: [default]
  0 artifacts copied, 10 already retrieved (0kB/18ms)
-------------------------------------------
Time: 2015-11-01 12:13:16
-------------------------------------------


-------------------------------------------
Time: 2015-11-01 12:13:17
-------------------------------------------


-------------------------------------------
Time: 2015-11-01 12:13:18
-------------------------------------------


-------------------------------------------
Time: 2015-11-01 12:13:19
-------------------------------------------
(u'a', 5)
(u'the', 5)
(u'11:50AM', 5)
(u'from', 5)
(u'This', 5)
(u'11:50:21.044374Sunday,', 1)
(u'message', 5)
(u'11:50:20.036422Sunday,', 1)
(u'11:50:22.051423Sunday,', 1)
(u'11:50:17.867309Sunday,', 1)
...


-------------------------------------------
Time: 2015-11-01 12:13:20
-------------------------------------------


-------------------------------------------
Time: 2015-11-01 12:13:21
-------------------------------------------
```

Exploring flume

Flume is a continuous ingestion system. It was originally designed to be a log aggregation system, but it evolved to handle any type of streaming event data.

Flume is a distributed, reliable, scalable, and available pipeline system for efficient collection, aggregation, and transport of large volumes of data. It has built-in support for contextual routing, filtering replication, and multiplexing. It is robust and fault tolerant, with tunable reliability mechanisms and many failover and recovery mechanisms. It uses a simple extensible data model that allows for real time analytic application.

Flume offers the following:

- Guaranteed delivery semantics
- Low latency reliable data transfer
- Declarative configuration with no coding required
- Extendable and customizable settings
- Integration with most commonly used end-points

The anatomy of Flume contains the following elements:

- **Event**: An event is the fundamental unit of data that is transported by Flume from source to destination. It is like a message with a byte array payload opaque to Flume and optional headers used for contextual routing.

- **Client**: A client produces and transmits events. A client decouples Flume from the data consumers. It is an entity that generates events and sends them to one or more agents. Custom client or Flume log4J append program or embedded application agent can be client.

- **Agent**: An agent is a container hosting sources, channels, sinks, and other elements that enable the transportation of events from one place to the other. It provides configuration, life cycle management and monitoring for hosted components. An agent is a physical Java virtual machine running Flume.

- **Source**: Source is the entity through which Flume receives events. Sources require at least one channel to function in order to either actively poll data or passively wait for data to be delivered to them. A variety of sources allow data to be collected, such as log4j logs and syslogs.

- **Sink**: Sink is the entity that drains data from the channel and delivers it to the next destination. A variety of sinks allow data to be streamed to a range of destinations. Sinks support serialization to user's format. One example is the HDFS sink that writes events to HDFS.

- **Channel**: Channel is the conduit between the source and the sink that buffers incoming events until drained by sinks. Sources feed events into the channel and the sinks drain the channel. Channels decouple the impedance of upstream and downstream systems. Burst of data upstream is damped by the channels. Failures downstream are transparently absorbed by the channels. Sizing the channel capacity to cope with these events is key to realizing these benefits. Channels offer two levels of persistence: either memory channel, which is volatile if the JVM crashes, or File channel backed by Write Ahead Log that stores the information to disk. Channels are fully transactional.

Let's illustrate all these concepts:

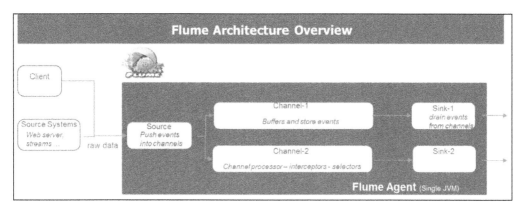

Developing data pipelines with Flume, Kafka, and Spark

Building resilient data pipeline leverages the learnings from the previous sections. We are plumbing together data ingestion and transport with Flume, data brokerage with a reliable and sophisticated publish and subscribe messaging system such as Kafka, and finally process computation on the fly using Spark Streaming.

The following diagram illustrates the composition of streaming data pipelines as sequence of *connect*, *collect*, *conduct*, *compose*, *consume*, *consign*, and *control* activities. These activities are configurable based on the use case:

- Connect establishes the binding with the streaming API.
- Collect creates collection threads.
- Conduct decouples the data producers from the consumers by creating a buffer queue or publish-subscribe mechanism.

- Compose is focused on processing the data.

- Consume provisions the processed data for the consuming systems. Consign takes care of the data persistence.

- Control caters to governance and monitoring of the systems, data, and applications.

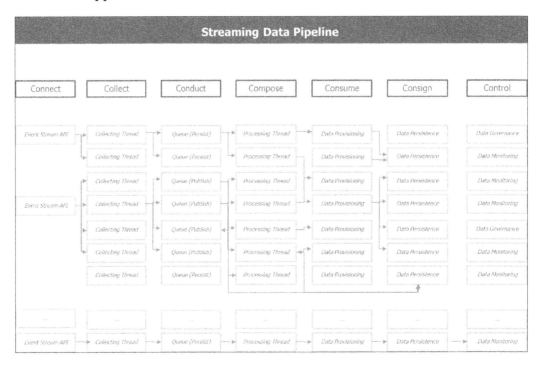

The following diagram illustrates the concepts of the streaming data pipelines with its key components: Spark Streaming, Kafka, Flume, and low latency databases. In the consuming or controlling applications, we are monitoring our systems in real time (depicted by a monitor) or sending real-time alerts (depicted by red lights) in case certain thresholds are crossed.

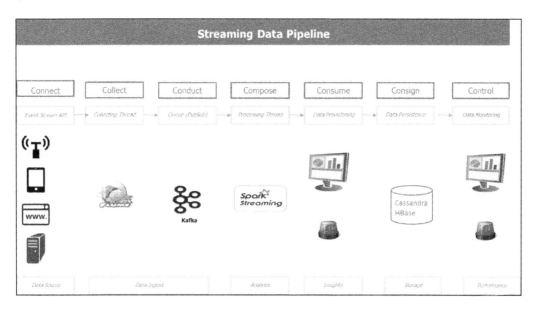

The following diagram illustrates Spark's unique ability to process in a single platform data in motion and data at rest while seamlessly interfacing with multiple persistence data stores as per the use case requirement.

This diagram brings in one unified whole all the concepts discussed up to now. The top part describes the streaming processing pipeline. The bottom part describes the batch processing pipeline. They both share a common persistence layer in the middle of the diagram depicting the various modes of persistence and serialization.

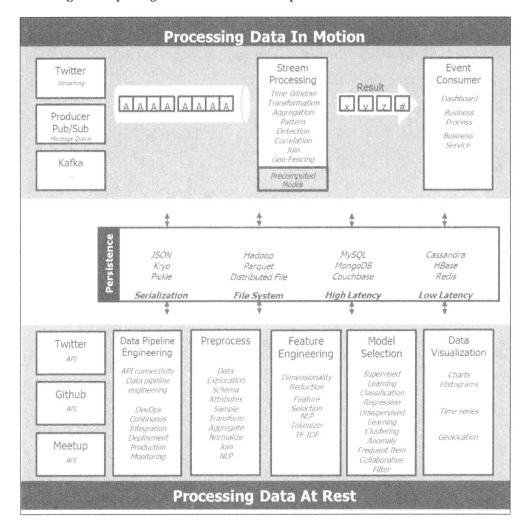

Closing remarks on the Lambda and Kappa architecture

Two architecture paradigms are currently in vogue: the Lambda and Kappa architectures.

Lambda is the brainchild of the Storm creator and main committer, Nathan Marz. It essentially advocates building a functional architecture on all data. The architecture has two branches. The first is a batch arm envisioned to be powered by Hadoop, where historical, high-latency, high-throughput data are pre-processed and made ready for consumption. The real-time arm is envisioned to be powered by Storm, and it processes incrementally streaming data, derives insights on the fly, and feeds aggregated information back to the batch storage.

Kappa is the brainchild of one the main committer of Kafka, Jay Kreps, and his colleagues at Confluent (previously at LinkedIn). It is advocating a full streaming pipeline, effectively implementing, at the enterprise level, the unified log enounced in the previous pages.

Understanding Lambda architecture

Lambda architecture combines batch and streaming data to provide a unified query mechanism on all available data. Lambda architecture envisions three layers: a batch layer where precomputed information are stored, a speed layer where real-time incremental information is processed as data streams, and finally the serving layer that merges batch and real-time views for ad hoc queries. The following diagram gives an overview of the Lambda architecture:

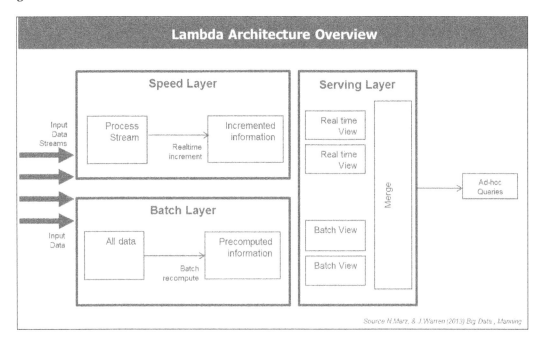

Understanding Kappa architecture

The Kappa architecture proposes to drive the full enterprise in streaming mode. The Kappa architecture arose from a critique from Jay Kreps and his colleagues at LinkedIn at the time. Since then, they moved and created Confluent with Apache Kafka as the main enabler of the Kappa architecture vision. The basic tenet is to move in all streaming mode with a Unified Log as the main backbone of the enterprise information architecture.

A Unified Log is a centralized enterprise structured log available for real-time subscription. All the organization's data is put in a central log for subscription. Records are numbered beginning with zero so that they are written. It is also known as a commit log or journal. The concept of the Unified Log is the central tenet of the Kappa architecture.

The properties of the unified log are as follows:

- **Unified**: There is a single deployment for the entire organization
- **Append only**: Events are immutable and are appended
- **Ordered**: Each event has a unique offset within a shard
- **Distributed**: For fault tolerance purpose, the unified log is distributed redundantly on a cluster of computers
- **Fast**: The systems ingests thousands of messages per second

The following screenshot captures the moment Jay Kreps announced his reservations about the Lambda architecture. His main reservation about the Lambda architecture is implementing the same job in two different systems, Hadoop and Storm, with each of their specific idiosyncrasies, and with all the complexities that come along with it. Kappa architecture processes the real-time data and reprocesses historical data in the same framework powered by Apache Kafka.

Summary

In this chapter, we laid out the foundations of streaming architecture apps and described their challenges, constraints, and benefits. We went under the hood and examined the inner working of Spark Streaming and how it fits with Spark Core and dialogues with Spark SQL and Spark MLlib. We illustrated the streaming concepts with TCP sockets, followed by live tweet ingestion and processing directly from the Twitter firehose. We discussed the notions of decoupling upstream data publishing from downstream data subscription and consumption using Kafka in order to maximize the resilience of the overall streaming architecture. We also discussed Flume—a reliable, flexible, and scalable data ingestion and transport pipeline system. The combination of Flume, Kafka, and Spark delivers unparalleled robustness, speed, and agility in an ever changing landscape. We closed the chapter with some remarks and observations on two streaming architectural paradigms, the Lambda and Kappa architectures.

The Lambda architecture combines batch and streaming data in a common query front-end. It was envisioned with Hadoop and Storm in mind initially. Spark has its own batch and streaming paradigms, and it offers a single environment with common code base to effectively bring this architecture paradigm to life.

The Kappa architecture promulgates the concept of the unified log, which creates an event-oriented architecture where all events in the enterprise are channeled in a centralized commit log that is available to all consuming systems in real time.

We are now ready for the visualization of the data collected and processed so far.

6
Visualizing Insights and Trends

So far, we have focused on the collection, analysis, and processing of data from Twitter. We have set the stage to use our data for visual rendering and extracting insights and trends. We will give a quick lay of the land about visualization tools in the Python ecosystem. We will highlight Bokeh as a powerful tool for rendering and viewing large datasets. Bokeh is part of the Python Anaconda Distribution ecosystem.

In this chapter, we will cover the following points:

- Gauging the key words and memes within a social network community using charts and wordcloud
- Mapping the most active location where communities are growing around certain themes or topics

Revisiting the data-intensive apps architecture

We have reached the final layer of the data-intensive apps architecture: the engagement layer. This layer focuses on how to synthesize, emphasize, and visualize the key context relevant information for the data consumers. A bunch of numbers in a console will not suffice to engage with end-users. It is critical to present the mass of information in a rapid, digestible, and attractive fashion.

The following diagram sets the context of the chapter's focus highlighting the engagement layer.

Data Intensive App Framework
Engagement Layer
Bokeh – Matplotlib – Seaborn – ggplot – mlpd3
Visualization (Charts, Time Series, Maps....)

Analytics Layer			
Spark SQL - Blaze	Spark MLlib	Spark GraphX	Spark Streaming
Exploration	*Machine Learning*	*Graph*	*Streaming*

Integration Layer
Blaze – SparkSQL - Pandas
Connect – Collect – Correct – Compose – Consume

Persistence Layer			
MySQL - PostgreSQL	Redis -HDFS	MongoDB	Cassandra
RDBMS	*K-V Store - File Systems*	*Document DB*	*Columnar DB*

Infrastructure Layer		
VirtualBox - Vagrant *Virtualization*	Amazon Web Services Anaconda Cluster *Scalability*	Docker/Chef/Puppet/Ansible *Continuous Integration*

For Python plotting and visualizations, we have quite a few tools and libraries. The most interesting and relevant ones for our purpose are the following:

- **Matplotlib** is the grandfather of the Python plotting libraries. Matplotlib was originally the brainchild of *John Hunter* who was an open source software proponent and established Matplotlib as one of the most prevalent plotting libraries both in the academic and the data scientific communities. Matplotlib allows the generation of plots, histograms, power spectra, bar charts, error charts, scatterplots, and so on. Examples can be found on the Matplotlib dedicated website at `http://matplotlib.org/examples/index.html`.

- **Seaborn**, developed by *Michael Waskom*, is a great library to quickly visualize statistical information. It is built on top of Matplotlib and integrates seamlessly with Pandas and the Python data stack, including Numpy. A gallery of graphs from Seaborn at `http://stanford.edu/~mwaskom/software/seaborn/examples/index.html` shows the potential of the library.

- **ggplot** is relatively new and aims to offer the equivalent of the famous ggplot2 from the R ecosystem for the Python data wranglers. It has the same look and feel of ggplot2 and uses the same grammar of graphics as expounded by Hadley Wickham. The ggplot the Python port is developed by the team at `yhat`. More information can be found at `http://ggplot.yhathq.com`.

- **D3.js** is a very popular, JavaScript library developed by *Mike Bostock*. **D3** stands for **Data Driven Documents** and brings data to life on any modern browser leveraging HTML, SVG, and CSS. It delivers dynamic, powerful, interactive visualizations by manipulating the DOM, the Document Object Model. The Python community could not wait to integrate D3 with Matplotlib. Under the impulse of Jake Vanderplas, mpld3 was created with the aim of bringing `matplotlib` to the browser. Examples graphics are hosted at the following address: `http://mpld3.github.io/index.html`.

- **Bokeh** aims to deliver high-performance interactivity over very large or streaming datasets whilst leveraging lot of the concepts of `D3.js` without the burden of writing some intimidating `javascript` and `css` code. Bokeh delivers dynamic visualizations on the browser with or without a server. It integrates seamlessly with Matplotlib, Seaborn and ggplot and renders beautifully in IPython notebooks or Jupyter notebooks. Bokeh is actively developed by the team at Continuum.io and is an integral part of the Anaconda Python data stack.

Bokeh server provides a full-fledged, dynamic plotting engine that materializes a reactive scene graph from JSON. It uses web sockets to keep state and update the HTML5 canvas using Backbone.js and Coffee-script under the hoods. Bokeh, as it is fueled by data in JSON, creates easy bindings for other languages such as R, Scala, and Julia.

This gives a high-level overview of the main plotting and visualization library. It is not exhaustive. Let's move to concrete examples of visualizations.

Preprocessing the data for visualization

Before jumping into the visualizations, we will do some preparatory work on the data harvested:

```
In [16]:
# Read harvested data stored in csv in a Panda DF
import pandas as pd
csv_in = '/home/an/spark/spark-1.5.0-bin-hadoop2.6/examples/AN_Spark/
data/unq_tweetstxt.csv'
pddf_in = pd.read_csv(csv_in, index_col=None, header=0, sep=';',
encoding='utf-8')
In [20]:
print('tweets pandas dataframe - count:', pddf_in.count())
print('tweets pandas dataframe - shape:', pddf_in.shape)
print('tweets pandas dataframe - colns:', pddf_in.columns)
('tweets pandas dataframe - count:', Unnamed: 0     7540
id              7540
created_at      7540
user_id         7540
user_name       7538
tweet_text      7540
dtype: int64)
('tweets pandas dataframe - shape:', (7540, 6))
('tweets pandas dataframe - colns:', Index([u'Unnamed: 0',
u'id', u'created_at', u'user_id', u'user_name', u'tweet_text'],
dtype='object'))
```

For the purpose of our visualization activity, we will use a dataset of 7,540 tweets. The key information is stored in the tweet_text column. We preview the data stored in the dataframe calling the head() function on the dataframe:

```
In [21]:
pddf_in.head()
Out[21]:
   Unnamed: 0   id   created_at   user_id   user_name   tweet_text
0    0    638830426971181057   Tue Sep 01 21:46:57 +0000 2015
3276255125    True Equality   ernestsgantt: BeyHiveInFrance: 9_A_6:
dreamint...
1    1    638830426727911424   Tue Sep 01 21:46:57 +0000 2015
3276255125    True Equality   ernestsgantt: BeyHiveInFrance:
PhuketDailyNews...
2    2    638830425402556417   Tue Sep 01 21:46:56 +0000 2015
3276255125    True Equality   ernestsgantt: BeyHiveInFrance: 9_A_6:
ernestsg...
```

```
3    3    638830424563716097    Tue Sep 01 21:46:56 +0000 2015
3276255125    True Equality    ernestsgantt: BeyHiveInFrance:
PhuketDailyNews...
4    4    638830422256816132    Tue Sep 01 21:46:56 +0000 2015
3276255125    True Equality    ernestsgantt: elsahel12: 9_A_6:
dreamintention...
```

We will now create some utility functions to clean up the tweet text and parse the twitter date. First, we import the Python regular expression regex library `re` and the time library to parse dates and time:

```
In [72]:
import re
import time
```

We create a dictionary of regex that will be compiled and then passed as function:

- **RT**: The first regex with key RT looks for the keyword RT at the beginning of the tweet text:

  ```
  re.compile(r'^RT'),
  ```

- **ALNUM**: The second regex with key ALNUM looks for words including alphanumeric characters and underscore sign preceded by the @ symbol in the tweet text:

  ```
  re.compile(r'(@[a-zA-Z0-9_]+)'),
  ```

- **HASHTAG**: The third regex with key HASHTAG looks for words including alphanumeric characters preceded by the # symbol in the tweet text:
  ```
  re.compile(r'(#[\w\d]+)'),
  ```

- **SPACES**: The fourth regex with key SPACES looks for blank or line space characters in the tweet text:
  ```
  re.compile(r'\s+'),
  ```

- **URL**: The fifth regex with key URL looks for `url` addresses including alphanumeric characters preceded with `https://` or `http://` markers in the tweet text:

  ```
  re.compile(r'([https://|http://]?[a-zA-Z\d\/]+[\.]+[a-zA-
  Z\d\/\.]+)')
  In [24]:
  regexp = {"RT": "^RT", "ALNUM": r"(@[a-zA-Z0-9_]+)",
            "HASHTAG": r"(#[\w\d]+)", "URL":
  r"([https://|http://]?[a-zA-Z\d\/]+[\.]+[a-zA-Z\d\/\.]+)",
            "SPACES":r"\s+"}
  ```

```
regexp = dict((key, re.compile(value)) for key, value in regexp.
items())
In [25]:
regexp
Out[25]:
{'ALNUM': re.compile(r'(@[a-zA-Z0-9_]+)'),
 'HASHTAG': re.compile(r'(#[\w\d]+)'),
 'RT': re.compile(r'^RT'),
 'SPACES': re.compile(r'\s+'),
 'URL': re.compile(r'([https://|http://]?[a-zA-Z\d\/]+[\.]+[a-zA-
Z\d\/\.]+)')}
```

We create a utility function to identify whether a tweet is a retweet or an original tweet:

```
In [77]:
def getAttributeRT(tweet):
    """ see if tweet is a RT """
    return re.search(regexp["RT"], tweet.strip()) != None
```

Then, we extract all user handles in a tweet:

```
def getUserHandles(tweet):
    """ given a tweet we try and extract all user handles"""
    return re.findall(regexp["ALNUM"], tweet)
```

We also extract all hashtags in a tweet:

```
def getHashtags(tweet):
    """ return all hashtags"""
    return re.findall(regexp["HASHTAG"], tweet)
```

Extract all URL links in a tweet as follows:

```
def getURLs(tweet):
    """ URL : [http://]?[\w\.?/]+"""
    return re.findall(regexp["URL"], tweet)
```

We strip all URL links and user handles preceded by @ sign in a tweet text. This function will be the basis of the wordcloud we will build soon:

```
def getTextNoURLsUsers(tweet):
    """ return parsed text terms stripped of URLs and User Names in
tweet text
        ' '.join(re.sub("(@[A-Za-z0-9]+)|([^0-9A-Za-z \t])|(\w+:\/\/\
S+)"," ",x).split()) """
    return ' '.join(re.sub("(@[A-Za-z0-9]+)|([^0-9A-Za-z \t])|(\
w+:\/\/\S+)|(RT)"," ", tweet).lower().split())
```

We label the data so we can create groups of datasets for the wordcloud:

```
def setTag(tweet):
    """ set tags to tweet_text based on search terms from tags_list"""
    tags_list = ['spark', 'python', 'clinton', 'trump', 'gaga',
'bieber']
    lower_text = tweet.lower()
    return filter(lambda x:x.lower() in lower_text,tags_list)
```

We parse the twitter date in the `yyyy-mm-dd hh:mm:ss` format:

```
def decode_date(s):
    """ parse Twitter date into format yyyy-mm-dd hh:mm:ss"""
    return time.strftime('%Y-%m-%d %H:%M:%S', time.strptime(s,'%a %b
%d %H:%M:%S +0000 %Y'))
```

We preview the data prior to processing:

```
In [43]:
pddf_in.columns
Out[43]:
Index([u'Unnamed: 0', u'id', u'created_at', u'user_id', u'user_name',
u'tweet_text'], dtype='object')
In [45]:
# df.drop([Column Name or list],inplace=True,axis=1)
pddf_in.drop(['Unnamed: 0'], inplace=True, axis=1)
In [46]:
pddf_in.head()
Out[46]:
   id   created_at   user_id   user_name   tweet_text
0   638830426971181057   Tue Sep 01 21:46:57 +0000 2015   3276255125
True Equality   ernestsgantt: BeyHiveInFrance: 9_A_6: dreamint...
1   638830426727911424   Tue Sep 01 21:46:57 +0000 2015   3276255125
True Equality   ernestsgantt: BeyHiveInFrance: PhuketDailyNews...
2   638830425402556417   Tue Sep 01 21:46:56 +0000 2015   3276255125
True Equality   ernestsgantt: BeyHiveInFrance: 9_A_6: ernestsg...
3   638830424563716097   Tue Sep 01 21:46:56 +0000 2015   3276255125
True Equality   ernestsgantt: BeyHiveInFrance: PhuketDailyNews...
4   638830422256816132   Tue Sep 01 21:46:56 +0000 2015   3276255125
True Equality   ernestsgantt: elsahel12: 9_A_6: dreamintention...
```

We create new dataframe columns by applying the utility functions described. We create a new column for htag, user handles, URLs, the text terms stripped from URLs, and unwanted characters and the labels. We finally parse the date:

```
In [82]:
pddf_in['htag'] = pddf_in.tweet_text.apply(getHashtags)
pddf_in['user_handles'] = pddf_in.tweet_text.apply(getUserHandles)
pddf_in['urls'] = pddf_in.tweet_text.apply(getURLs)
pddf_in['txt_terms'] = pddf_in.tweet_text.apply(getTextNoURLsUsers)
pddf_in['search_grp'] = pddf_in.tweet_text.apply(setTag)
pddf_in['date'] = pddf_in.created_at.apply(decode_date)
```

The following code gives a quick snapshot of the newly generated dataframe:

```
In [83]:
pddf_in[2200:2210]
Out[83]:
   id    created_at    user_id    user_name    tweet_text    htag    urls
ptxt    tgrp    date    user_handles    txt_terms    search_grp
2200    638242693374681088    Mon Aug 31 06:51:30 +0000 2015    19525954
CENATIC    El impacto de @ApacheSpark en el procesamiento...
[#sparkSpecial]    [://t.co/4PQmJNuEJB]    el impacto de en el
procesamiento de datos y e...    [spark]    2015-08-31 06:51:30    [@
ApacheSpark]    el impacto de en el procesamiento de datos y e...
[spark]
2201    638238014695575552    Mon Aug 31 06:32:55 +0000 2015    51115854
Nawfal    Real Time Streaming with Apache Spark\nhttp://...    [#IoT,
#SmartMelboune, #BigData, #Apachespark]    [://t.co/GW5PaqwVab]    real
time streaming with apache spark iot smar...    [spark]    2015-08-
31 06:32:55    []    real time streaming with apache spark iot smar...
[spark]
2202    638236084124516352    Mon Aug 31 06:25:14 +0000 2015    62885987
Mithun Katti    RT @differentsachin: Spark the flame of digita...
[#IBMHackathon, #SparkHackathon, #ISLconnectIN...    []    spark
the flame of digital india ibmhackathon ...    [spark]    2015-08-
31 06:25:14    [@differentsachin, @ApacheSpark]    spark the flame of
digital india ibmhackathon ...    [spark]
2203    638234734649176064    Mon Aug 31 06:19:53 +0000 2015    140462395
solaimurugan v    Installing @ApacheMahout with @ApacheSpark 1.4...
[]    [1.4.1, ://t.co/3c5dGbfaZe.]    installing with 1 4 1 got many
more issue whil...    [spark]    2015-08-31 06:19:53    [@ApacheMahout,
@ApacheSpark]    installing with 1 4 1 got many more issue whil...
[spark]
```

```
2204    638233517307072512    Mon Aug 31 06:15:02 +0000 2015
2428473836    Ralf Heineke    RT @RomeoKienzler: Join me @velocityconf
on #m...    [#machinelearning, #devOps, #Bl]    [://t.co/U5xL7pYEmF]
join me on machinelearning based devops operat...    [spark]    2015-08-
31 06:15:02    [@RomeoKienzler, @velocityconf, @ApacheSpark]    join me
on machinelearning based devops operat...    [spark]
2205    638230184848687106    Mon Aug 31 06:01:48 +0000 2015    289355748
Akim Boyko    RT @databricks: Watch live today at 10am PT is...
[]    [1.5, ://t.co/16cix6ASti]    watch live today at 10am pt is 1
5 presented b...    [spark]    2015-08-31 06:01:48    [@databricks, @
ApacheSpark, @databricks, @pwen...    watch live today at 10am pt is 1
5 presented b...    [spark]
2206    638227830443110400    Mon Aug 31 05:52:27 +0000 2015    145001241
sachin aggarwal    Spark the flame of digital India @ #IBMHackath...
[#IBMHackathon, #SparkHackathon, #ISLconnectIN...    [://t.co/
C1AO3uNexe]    spark the flame of digital india ibmhackathon ...
[spark]    2015-08-31 05:52:27    [@ApacheSpark]    spark the flame of
digital india ibmhackathon ...    [spark]
2207    638227031268810752    Mon Aug 31 05:49:16 +0000 2015    145001241
sachin aggarwal    RT @pravin_gadakh: Imagine, innovate and Igni...
[#IBMHackathon, #ISLconnectIN2015]    []    gadakh imagine innovate
and ignite digital ind...    [spark]    2015-08-31 05:49:16    [@pravin_
gadakh, @ApacheSpark]    gadakh imagine innovate and ignite digital
ind...    [spark]
2208    638224591920336896    Mon Aug 31 05:39:35 +0000 2015    494725634
IBM Asia Pacific    RT @sachinparmar: Passionate about Spark?? Hav...
[#IBMHackathon, #ISLconnectIN]    [India..]    passionate about spark
have dreams of clean sa...    [spark]    2015-08-31 05:39:35    [@
sachinparmar]    passionate about spark have dreams of clean sa...
[spark]
2209    638223327467692032    Mon Aug 31 05:34:33 +0000 2015
3158070968    Open Source India    "Game Changer" #ApacheSpark speeds up
#bigdata...    [#ApacheSpark, #bigdata]    [://t.co/ieTQ9ocMim]    game
changer apachespark speeds up bigdata pro...    [spark]    2015-08-
31 05:34:33    []    game changer apachespark speeds up bigdata pro...
[spark]
```

We save the processed information in a CSV format. We have 7,540 records and 13 columns. In your case, the output will vary according to the dataset you chose:

```
In [84]:
f_name = '/home/an/spark/spark-1.5.0-bin-hadoop2.6/examples/AN_Spark/
data/unq_tweets_processed.csv'
pddf_in.to_csv(f_name, sep=';', encoding='utf-8', index=False)
In [85]:
pddf_in.shape
Out[85]:
(7540, 13)
```

Gauging words, moods, and memes at a glance

We are now ready to proceed with building the wordclouds which will give us a sense of the important words carried in those tweets. We will create wordclouds for the datasets harvested. Wordclouds extract the top words in a list of words and create a scatterplot of the words where the size of the word is correlated to its frequency. The more frequent the word in the dataset, the bigger will be the font size in the wordcloud rendering. They include three very different themes and two competing or analogous entities. Our first theme is obviously data processing and analytics, with Apache Spark and Python as our entities. Our second theme is the 2016 presidential election campaign, with the two contenders: Hilary Clinton and Donald Trump. Our last theme is the world of pop music with Justin Bieber and Lady Gaga as the two exponents.

Setting up wordcloud

We will illustrate the programming steps by analyzing the spark related tweets. We load the data and preview the dataframe:

```
In [21]:
import pandas as pd
csv_in = '/home/an/spark/spark-1.5.0-bin-hadoop2.6/examples/AN_Spark/
data/spark_tweets.csv'
tspark_df = pd.read_csv(csv_in, index_col=None, header=0, sep=',',
encoding='utf-8')
In [3]:
tspark_df.head(3)
Out[3]:
   id    created_at    user_id    user_name    tweet_text    htag    urls
ptxt    tgrp    date    user_handles    txt_terms    search_grp
0    638818911773856000    Tue Sep 01 21:01:11 +0000 2015    2511247075
Noor Din    RT @kdnuggets: R leads RapidMiner, Python catc...    [#KDN]
[://t.co/3bsaTT7eUs]    r leads rapidminer python catches up big data
...    [spark, python]    2015-09-01 21:01:11    [@kdnuggets]    r leads
rapidminer python catches up big data ...    [spark, python]
1    622142176768737000    Fri Jul 17 20:33:48 +0000 2015    24537879
IBM Cloudant    Be one of the first to sign-up for IBM Analyti...
[#ApacheSpark, #SparkInsight]    [://t.co/C5TZpetVA6, ://t.co/
R1L29DePaQ]    be one of the first to sign up for ibm analyti...
[spark]    2015-07-17 20:33:48    []    be one of the first to sign up
for ibm analyti...    [spark]
```

```
2    622140453069169000    Fri Jul 17 20:26:57 +0000 2015    515145898
Arno Candel   Nice article on #apachespark, #hadoop and #dat...
[#apachespark, #hadoop, #datascience]   [://t.co/IyF44pV0f3]    nice
article on apachespark hadoop and datasci...   [spark]   2015-07-
17 20:26:57   [@h2oai]    nice article on apachespark hadoop and
datasci...   [spark]
```

 The wordcloud library we will use is the one developed by Andreas Mueller and hosted on his GitHub account at `https://github.com/amueller/word_cloud`.

The library requires **PIL** (short for **Python Imaging Library**). PIL is easily installable by invoking `conda install pil`. PIL is a complex library to install and is not yet ported on Python 3.4, so we need to run a Python 2.7+ environment to be able to see our wordcloud:

```
#
# Install PIL (does not work with Python 3.4)
#
an@an-VB:~$ conda install pil

Fetching package metadata: ....
Solving package specifications: .................
Package plan for installation in environment /home/an/anaconda:
```

The following packages will be downloaded:

```
package                    |             build
---------------------------|-----------------
libpng-1.6.17              |                 0        214 KB
freetype-2.5.5             |                 0        2.2 MB
conda-env-2.4.4            |           py27_0         24 KB
pil-1.1.7                  |           py27_2        650 KB
------------------------------------------------------------
                                       Total:        3.0 MB
```

The following packages will be UPDATED:

```
conda-env: 2.4.2-py27_0 --> 2.4.4-py27_0
freetype:  2.5.2-0      --> 2.5.5-0
libpng:    1.5.13-1     --> 1.6.17-0
pil:       1.1.7-py27_1 --> 1.1.7-py27_2

Proceed ([y]/n)? y
```

Next, we install the wordcloud library:

```
#
# Install wordcloud
# Andreas Mueller
# https://github.com/amueller/word_cloud/blob/master/wordcloud/
wordcloud.py
#

an@an-VB:~$ pip install wordcloud
Collecting wordcloud
  Downloading wordcloud-1.1.3.tar.gz (163kB)
    100% |█████████████████████████████████| 163kB 548kB/s
Building wheels for collected packages: wordcloud
  Running setup.py bdist_wheel for wordcloud
  Stored in directory: /home/an/.cache/pip/wheels/32/a9/74/58e379e5dc6
14bfd9dd9832d67608faac9b2bc6c194d6f6df5
Successfully built wordcloud
Installing collected packages: wordcloud
Successfully installed wordcloud-1.1.3
```

Creating wordclouds

At this stage, we are ready to invoke the wordcloud program with the generated list of terms from the tweet text.

Let's get started with the wordcloud program by first calling `%matplotlib` inline to display the wordcloud in our notebook:

```
In [4]:
%matplotlib inline
In [11]:
```

We convert the dataframe `txt_terms` column into a list of words. We make sure it is all converted into the `str` type to avoid any bad surprises and check the list's first four records:

```
len(tspark_df['txt_terms'].tolist())
Out[11]:
2024
In [22]:
tspark_ls_str = [str(t) for t in tspark_df['txt_terms'].tolist()]
In [14]:
len(tspark_ls_str)
Out[14]:
```

```
2024
In [15]:
tspark_ls_str[:4]
Out[15]:
['r leads rapidminer python catches up big data tools grow spark
ignites kdn',
 'be one of the first to sign up for ibm analytics for apachespark
today sparkinsight',
 'nice article on apachespark hadoop and datascience',
 'spark 101 running spark and mapreduce together in production
hadoopsummit2015 apachespark altiscale']
```

We first call the Matplotlib and the wordcloud libraries:

```
import matplotlib.pyplot as plt
from wordcloud import WordCloud, STOPWORDS
```

From the input list of terms, we create a unified string of terms separated by a whitespace as the input to the wordcloud program. The wordcloud program removes stopwords:

```
# join tweets to a single string
words = ' '.join(tspark_ls_str)

# create wordcloud
wordcloud = WordCloud(
                    # remove stopwords
                    stopwords=STOPWORDS,
                    background_color='black',
                    width=1800,
                    height=1400
                    ).generate(words)


# render wordcloud image
plt.imshow(wordcloud)
plt.axis('off')

# save wordcloud image on disk
plt.savefig('./spark_tweets_wordcloud_1.png', dpi=300)

# display image in Jupyter notebook
plt.show()
```

Here, we can visualize the wordclouds for Apache Spark and Python. Clearly, in the case of Spark, *Hadoop*, *big data*, and *analytics* are the memes, while Python recalls the root of its name Monty Python with a strong focus on *developer*, *apache spark*, and programming with some hints to java and ruby.

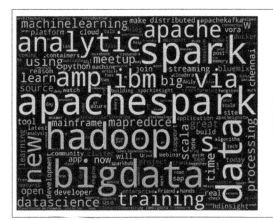

We can also get a glimpse in the following wordclouds of the words preoccupying the North American 2016 presidential election candidates: Hilary Clinton and Donald Trump. Seemingly Hilary Clinton is overshadowed by the presence of her opponents Donald Trump and Bernie Sanders, while Trump is heavily centered only on himself:

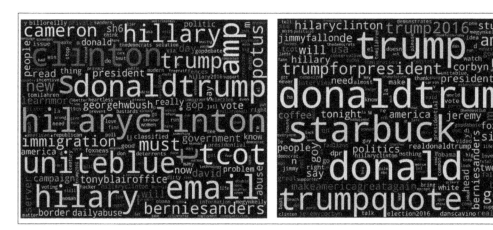

Interestingly, in the case of Justin Bieber and Lady Gaga, the word *love* appears. In the case of Bieber, *follow* and *belieber* are key words, while *diet*, *weight loss*, and *fashion* are the preoccupations for the Lady Gaga crowd.

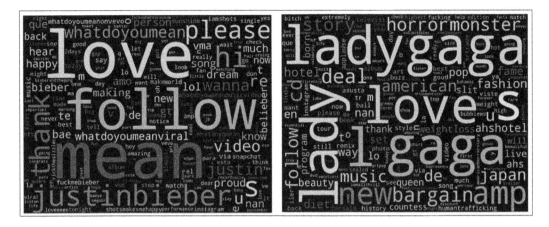

Geo-locating tweets and mapping meetups

Now, we will dive into the creation of interactive maps with Bokeh. First, we create a world map where we geo-locate sample tweets and, on moving our mouse over these locations, we can see the users and their respective tweets in a hover box.

The second map is focused on mapping upcoming meetups in London. It could be an interactive map that would act as a reminder of date, time, and location for upcoming meetups in a specific city.

Geo-locating tweets

The objective is to create a world map scatter plot of the locations of important tweets on the map, and the tweets and authors are revealed on hovering over these points. We will go through three steps to build this interactive visualization:

1. Create the background world map by first loading a dictionary of all the world country boundaries defined by their respective longitude and latitudes.

2. Load the important tweets we wish to geo-locate with their respective coordinates and authors.

3. Finally, scatter plot on the world map the tweets coordinates and activate the hover tool to visualize interactively the tweets and author on the highlighted dots on the map.

In step one, we create a Python list called data that will contain all the world countries boundaries with their respective latitude and longitude:

```
In [4]:
#
# This module exposes geometry data for World Country Boundaries.
#
import csv
import codecs
import gzip
import xml.etree.cElementTree as et
import os
from os.path import dirname, join

nan = float('NaN')
__file__ = os.getcwd()

data = {}
with gzip.open(join(dirname(__file__), 'AN_Spark/data/World_Country_
Boundaries.csv.gz')) as f:
    decoded = codecs.iterdecode(f, "utf-8")
    next(decoded)
    reader = csv.reader(decoded, delimiter=',', quotechar='"')
    for row in reader:
        geometry, code, name = row
        xml = et.fromstring(geometry)
        lats = []
        lons = []
        for i, poly in enumerate(xml.findall('.//outerBoundaryIs/
LinearRing/coordinates')):
            if i > 0:
                lats.append(nan)
                lons.append(nan)
            coords = (c.split(',')[:2] for c in poly.text.split())
            lat, lon = list(zip(*[(float(lat), float(lon)) for lon,
lat in
                coords]))
            lats.extend(lat)
            lons.extend(lon)
        data[code] = {
            'name'  : name,
            'lats'  : lats,
            'lons'  : lons,
        }
```

```
In [5]:
len(data)
Out[5]:
235
```

In step two, we load a sample set of important tweets that we wish to visualize with their respective geo-location information:

```
In [69]:
# data
#
#
In [8]:
import pandas as pd
csv_in = '/home/an/spark/spark-1.5.0-bin-hadoop2.6/examples/AN_Spark/
data/spark_tweets_20.csv'
t20_df = pd.read_csv(csv_in, index_col=None, header=0, sep=',',
encoding='utf-8')
In [9]:
t20_df.head(3)
Out[9]:
    id  created_at  user_id    user_name    tweet_text  htag    urls
ptxt    tgrp    date    user_handles    txt_terms    search_grp  lat
lon
0   638818911773856000  Tue Sep 01 21:01:11 +0000 2015  2511247075
Noor Din    RT @kdnuggets: R leads RapidMiner, Python catc...   [#KDN]
[://t.co/3bsaTT7eUs]    r leads rapidminer python catches up big data
...     [spark, python]     2015-09-01 21:01:11     [@kdnuggets]    r
leads rapidminer python catches up big data ...    [spark, python]
37.279518    -121.867905
1   622142176768737000  Fri Jul 17 20:33:48 +0000 2015  24537879
IBM Cloudant    Be one of the first to sign-up for IBM Analyti...
[#ApacheSpark, #SparkInsight]   [://t.co/C5TZpetVA6, ://t.co/
R1L29DePaQ]    be one of the first to sign up for ibm analyti...
[spark]     2015-07-17 20:33:48     []  be one of the first to sign up
for ibm analyti...  [spark]     37.774930    -122.419420
2   622140453069169000  Fri Jul 17 20:26:57 +0000 2015  515145898
Arno Candel     Nice article on #apachespark, #hadoop and #dat...
[#apachespark, #hadoop, #datascience]   [://t.co/IyF44pV0f3]    nice
article on apachespark hadoop and datasci...    [spark]     2015-07-
17 20:26:57     [@h2oai]    nice article on apachespark hadoop and
datasci...  [spark]     51.500130    -0.126305
In [98]:
len(t20_df.user_id.unique())
Out[98]:
19
In [17]:
```

```
t20_geo = t20_df[['date', 'lat', 'lon', 'user_name', 'tweet_text']]
In [24]:
#
t20_geo.rename(columns={'user_name':'user', 'tweet_text':'text' },
inplace=True)
In [25]:
t20_geo.head(4)
Out[25]:
    date      lat      lon      user      text
0   2015-09-01 21:01:11    37.279518    -121.867905    Noor Din    RT
@kdnuggets: R leads RapidMiner, Python catc...
1   2015-07-17 20:33:48    37.774930    -122.419420    IBM Cloudant
Be one of the first to sign-up for IBM Analyti...
2   2015-07-17 20:26:57    51.500130    -0.126305   Arno Candel
Nice article on #apachespark, #hadoop and #dat...
3   2015-07-17 19:35:31    51.500130    -0.126305    Ira Michael
Blonder      Spark 101: Running Spark and #MapReduce togeth...
In [22]:
df = t20_geo
#
```

In step three, we first imported all the necessary Bokeh libraries. We will instantiate the output in the Jupyter Notebook. We get the world countries boundary information loaded. We get the geo-located tweet data. We instantiate the Bokeh interactive tools such as wheel and box zoom as well as the hover tool.

```
In [29]:
#
# Bokeh Visualization of tweets on world map
#
from bokeh.plotting import *
from bokeh.models import HoverTool, ColumnDataSource
from collections import OrderedDict

# Output in Jupiter Notebook
output_notebook()

# Get the world map
world_countries = data.copy()

# Get the tweet data
tweets_source = ColumnDataSource(df)

# Create world map
```

```
countries_source = ColumnDataSource(data= dict(
    countries_xs=[world_countries[code]['lons'] for code in world_
countries],
    countries_ys=[world_countries[code]['lats'] for code in world_
countries],
    country = [world_countries[code]['name'] for code in world_
countries],
))


# Instantiate the bokeh interactive tools
TOOLS="pan,wheel_zoom,box_zoom,reset,resize,hover,save"
```

We are now ready to layer the various elements gathered into an object figure called **p**. Define the title, width, and height of **p**. Attach the tools. Create the world map background by patches with a light background color and borders. Scatter plot the tweets according to their respective geo-coordinates. Then, activate the hover tool with the users and their respective tweet. Finally, render the picture on the browser. The code is as follows:

```
# Instantiante the figure object
p = figure(
    title="%s tweets " %(str(len(df.index))),
    title_text_font_size="20pt",
    plot_width=1000,
    plot_height=600,
    tools=TOOLS)

# Create world patches background
p.patches(xs="countries_xs", ys="countries_ys", source = countries_
source, fill_color="#F1EEF6", fill_alpha=0.3,
        line_color="#999999", line_width=0.5)

# Scatter plots by longitude and latitude
p.scatter(x="lon", y="lat", source=tweets_source, fill_
color="#FF0000", line_color="#FF0000")
#

# Activate hover tool with user and corresponding tweet information
hover = p.select(dict(type=HoverTool))
hover.point_policy = "follow_mouse"
hover.tooltips = OrderedDict([
    ("user", "@user"),
    ("tweet", "@text"),
])

# Render the figure on the browser
```

```
show(p)
BokehJS successfully loaded.

inspect

#
#
```

The following code gives an overview of the world map with the red dots representing the locations of the tweets' origins:

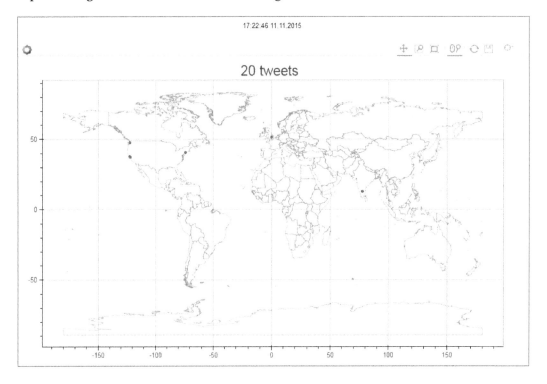

We can hover on a specific dot to reveal the tweets in that location:

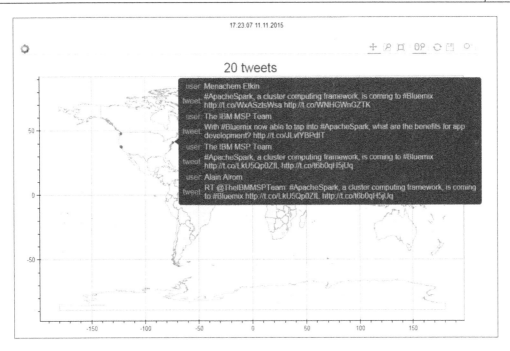

We can zoom into a specific location:

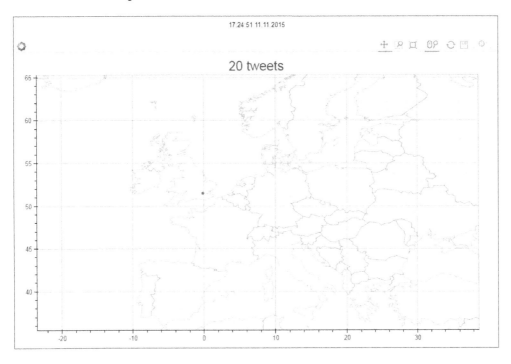

Finally, we can reveal the tweets in the given zoomed-in location:

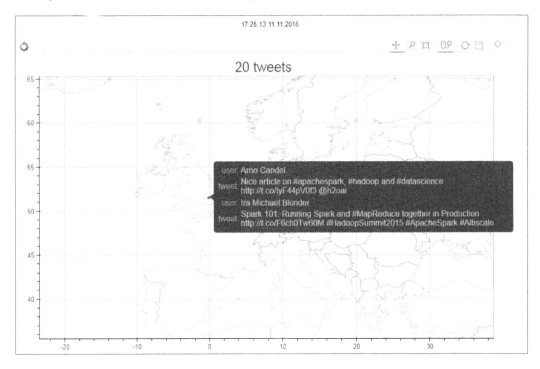

Displaying upcoming meetups on Google Maps

Now, our objective is to focus on upcoming meetups in London. We are mapping three meetups **Data Science London**, **Apache Spark**, and **Machine Learning**. We embed a Google Map within a Bokeh visualization and geo-locate the three meetups according to their coordinates and get information such as the name of the upcoming event for each meetup with a hover tool.

First, import all the necessary Bokeh libraries:

```
In [ ]:
#
# Bokeh Google Map Visualization of London with hover on specific
points
#
#
from __future__ import print_function
```

```
from bokeh.browserlib import view
from bokeh.document import Document
from bokeh.embed import file_html
from bokeh.models.glyphs import Circle
from bokeh.models import (
    GMapPlot, Range1d, ColumnDataSource,
    PanTool, WheelZoomTool, BoxSelectTool,
    HoverTool, ResetTool,
    BoxSelectionOverlay, GMapOptions)
from bokeh.resources import INLINE

x_range = Range1d()
y_range = Range1d()
```

We will instantiate the Google Map that will act as the substrate upon which our Bokeh visualization will be layered:

```
# JSON style string taken from: https://snazzymaps.com/style/1/pale-
dawn
map_options = GMapOptions(lat=51.50013, lng=-0.126305, map_
type="roadmap", zoom=13, styles="""
[{"featureType":"administrative","elementType":"all","stylers":[{"visi
bility":"on"},{"lightness":33}]},
 {"featureType":"landscape","elementType":"all","stylers":[{"color":"
#f2e5d4"}]},
 {"featureType":"poi.park","elementType":"geometry","stylers":[{"color
":"#c5dac6"}]},
 {"featureType":"poi.park","elementType":"labels","stylers":[{"visibil
ity":"on"},{"lightness":20}]},
 {"featureType":"road","elementType":"all","stylers":[{"lightne
ss":20}]},
 {"featureType":"road.highway","elementType":"geometry","stylers":[{"c
olor":"#c5c6c6"}]},
 {"featureType":"road.arterial","elementType":"geometry","stylers":[{"
color":"#e4d7c6"}]},
 {"featureType":"road.local","elementType":"geometry","stylers":[{"col
or":"#fbfaf7"}]},
 {"featureType":"water","elementType":"all","stylers":[{"visibility":"
on"},{"color":"#acbcc9"}]}]
""")
```

Instantiate the Bokeh object plot from the class `GMapPlot` with the dimensions and map options from the previous step:

```
# Instantiate Google Map Plot
plot = GMapPlot(
    x_range=x_range, y_range=y_range,
    map_options=map_options,
    title="London Meetups"
)
```

Bring in the information from our three meetups we wish to plot and get the information by hovering above the respective coordinates:

```
source = ColumnDataSource(
    data=dict(
        lat=[51.49013, 51.50013, 51.51013],
        lon=[-0.130305, -0.126305, -0.120305],
        fill=['orange', 'blue', 'green'],
        name=['LondonDataScience', 'Spark', 'MachineLearning'],
        text=['Graph Data & Algorithms','Spark Internals','Deep
Learning on Spark']
    )
)
```

Define the dots to be drawn on the Google Map:

```
circle = Circle(x="lon", y="lat", size=15, fill_color="fill", line_
color=None)
plot.add_glyph(source, circle)
```

Define the stings for the Bokeh tools to be used in this visualization:

```
# TOOLS="pan,wheel_zoom,box_zoom,reset,hover,save"
pan = PanTool()
wheel_zoom = WheelZoomTool()
box_select = BoxSelectTool()
reset = ResetTool()
hover = HoverTool()
# save = SaveTool()

plot.add_tools(pan, wheel_zoom, box_select, reset, hover)
overlay = BoxSelectionOverlay(tool=box_select)
plot.add_layout(overlay)
```

Activate the `hover` tool with the information that will be carried:

```
hover = plot.select(dict(type=HoverTool))
hover.point_policy = "follow_mouse"
hover.tooltips = OrderedDict([
    ("Name", "@name"),
    ("Text", "@text"),
    ("(Long, Lat)", "(@lon, @lat)"),
])

show(plot)
```

Render the plot that gives a pretty good view of London:

Once we hover on a highlighted dot, we can get the information of the given meetup:

Full smooth zooming capability is preserved, as the following screenshot shows:

Summary

In this chapter, we focused on few visualization techniques. We saw how to build wordclouds and their intuitive power to reveal, at a glance, lots of the key words, moods, and memes carried through thousands of tweets.

We then discussed interactive mapping visualizations using Bokeh. We built a world map from the ground up and created a scatter plot of critical tweets. Once the map was rendered on the browser, we could interactively hover from dot to dot and reveal the tweets originating from different parts of the world.

Our final visualization was focused on mapping upcoming meetups in London on Spark, data science, and machine learning and their respective topics, making a beautiful interactive visualization with an actual Google Map.

Index

Thank you for buying
Spark for Python Developers

About Packt Publishing

Packt, pronounced 'packed', published its first book, *Mastering phpMyAdmin for Effective MySQL Management*, in April 2004, and subsequently continued to specialize in publishing highly focused books on specific technologies and solutions.

Our books and publications share the experiences of your fellow IT professionals in adapting and customizing today's systems, applications, and frameworks. Our solution-based books give you the knowledge and power to customize the software and technologies you're using to get the job done. Packt books are more specific and less general than the IT books you have seen in the past. Our unique business model allows us to bring you more focused information, giving you more of what you need to know, and less of what you don't.

Packt is a modern yet unique publishing company that focuses on producing quality, cutting-edge books for communities of developers, administrators, and newbies alike. For more information, please visit our website at www.packtpub.com.

About Packt Open Source

In 2010, Packt launched two new brands, Packt Open Source and Packt Enterprise, in order to continue its focus on specialization. This book is part of the Packt Open Source brand, home to books published on software built around open source licenses, and offering information to anybody from advanced developers to budding web designers. The Open Source brand also runs Packt's Open Source Royalty Scheme, by which Packt gives a royalty to each open source project about whose software a book is sold.

Writing for Packt

We welcome all inquiries from people who are interested in authoring. Book proposals should be sent to author@packtpub.com. If your book idea is still at an early stage and you would like to discuss it first before writing a formal book proposal, then please contact us; one of our commissioning editors will get in touch with you.

We're not just looking for published authors; if you have strong technical skills but no writing experience, our experienced editors can help you develop a writing career, or simply get some additional reward for your expertise.

Machine Learning with Spark

ISBN: 978-1-78328-851-9   Paperback: 338 pages

Create scalable machine learning applications to power a modern data-driven business using Spark

1. A practical tutorial with real-world use cases allowing you to develop your own machine learning systems with Spark.

2. Combine various techniques and models into an intelligent machine learning system.

3. Use SparkTs powerful tools to load, analyze, clean, and transform your data.

Learning Real-time Processing with Spark Streaming

ISBN: 978-1-78398-766-5   Paperback: 202 pages

Building scalable and fault-tolerant streaming applications made easy with Spark streaming

1. Process live data streams more efficiently with better fault recovery using Spark Streaming.

2. Implement and deploy real-time log file analysis.

3. Learn about integration with Advance Spark Libraries – GraphX, Spark SQL, and MLib.

Please check **www.PacktPub.com** for information on our titles

Spark Cookbook

ISBN: 978-1-78398-706-1   Paperback: 226 pages

Over 60 recipes on Spark, covering Spark Core, Spark SQL, Spark Streaming, MLlib, and GraphX libraries

1. Become an expert at graph processing using GraphX.

2. Use Apache Spark as your single big data compute platform and master its libraries.

3. Learn with recipes that can be run on a single machine as well as on a production cluster of thousands of machines.

Practical Data Science Cookbook

ISBN: 978-1-78398-024-6   Paperback: 396 pages

89 hands-on recipes to help you complete real-world data science projects in R and Python

1. Learn about the data science pipeline and use it to acquire, clean, analyze, and visualize data.

2. Understand critical concepts in data science in the context of multiple projects.

3. Expand your numerical programming skills through step-by-step code examples and learn more about the robust features of R and Python.

Please check **www.PacktPub.com** for information on our titles

Lightning Source UK Ltd.
Milton Keynes UK
UKOW05f1821200416

272654UK00002B/6/P